REPRESENTING RADICALS

A GUIDE FOR LAWYERS AND MOVEMENTS

T0126299

Anarchist Interventions | 08

ISBN: 978-1-84935-416-5
E-ISBN: 978-1-84935-417-2
Library of Congress Control Number: 2020946129

AK Press   AK Press
370 Ryan Ave. #100   33 Tower St.
Chico, CA 95973   Edinburgh EH6 7BN
USA   Scotland
www.akpress.org   www.akuk.com
akpress@akpress.org   akuk@akpress.org

Institute for Anarchist Studies
PO Box 90454
Portland, OR 97290
www.anarchiststudies.org

Please contact us to request the latest AK Press distribution catalog,
which features books, pamphlets, zines, and stylish apparel published
and/or distributed by AK Press. Alternatively, visit our websites for
the complete catalog, latest news, and secure ordering.

Series design by Josh MacPhee / justseeds.org
Cover illustration by Cece McGuire and interior artwork
by Roger Peet
Printed in the USA on acid-free, recycled paper

REPRESENTING RADICALS

A GUIDE FOR LAWYERS AND MOVEMENTS

Tilted Scales Collective

Foreword by Lauren Regan

AK Press / Institute for Anarchist Studies | 2021

Anarchist Interventions:

An IAS/AK Press Book Series

Radical ideas can open up spaces for radical actions by illuminating hierarchical power relations and drawing out possibilities for liberatory social transformations. The Anarchist Intervention series—a collaborative project between the Institute for Anarchist Studies (IAS) and AK Press—strives to contribute to the development of relevant, vital anarchist theory and analysis by intervening in contemporary discussions. Works in this series will look at twenty-first-century social conditions—including social structures and oppression, their historical trajectories, and new forms of domination, to name a few—as well as reveal opportunities for different tomorrows premised on horizontal, egalitarian forms of self-organization.

Given that anarchism has become the dominant tendency within revolutionary milieus and movements today, it is crucial that anarchists explore current phenomena, strategies, and visions in a much more rigorous, serious manner. Each title in this series, then, will feature a present-day anarchist voice, with the aim, over time, of publishing a variety of perspectives. The series' multifaceted goals are to cultivate anarchist thought so as to better inform anarchist practice, encourage a culture of public intellectuals and constructive debate within anarchism, introduce new generations to anarchism, and offer insights into today's world and potentialities for a freer society.

Contents

Foreword

I became a movement lawyer in 1997, upon graduating from law school in Eugene, Oregon. The *Chicago Tribune* described the city at that time as a "laboratory for revolutionaries bent on knocking the legs out from under modern society."[1] I had been active in the environmental and animal rights movements before law school, and found it to be a fun time to be a young twenty-something activist lawyer with lots to learn and experience in the run up to the World Trade Organization protests and the burgeoning anti-globalization/anti-capitalist protest movement on the "Left" Coast. "Trial by fire" took on new meaning for me in the early 2000s as my friends and community began to realize they were being heavily surveilled, policed, and physically attacked by the State in the wake of the "Green Scare."[2] FBI knock-and-talks became frequent. Grand juries were threatened, and paranoia grew. I immediately researched who of my many lawyer-mentors were experienced in political grand jury resistance. There were very few. I traveled to various locations around the country to meet with that handful of lawyers to learn their stories and get their tactical advice—and reassurance that I would not (likely) be jailed alongside my clients.

This journey was scary and reassuring at the same time. It was also absolutely essential for me to learn at the knee of other political movement lawyers how to respond to the feds and communicate with my clients. Likewise, these discussions were essential for me to learn how to provide my clients with legal advice that was real in terms of the potential consequences of their decisions, that was in alignment with the movement ideologies we shared, and that would best armor me as a lawyer from being targeted by the feds myself.

And then indictments and arrests hit in what was dubbed "Operation Backfire" with unprecedented threats of life plus 1,115 years in prison for economic sabotage.[3] About half of the Earth Liberation Front and Animal Liberation Front cell members who were arrested caved and became despicable snitches. I represented, supported, advised, and provided media interviews on behalf of the noncooperating defendants who ended up doing about a year and a half more than the similarly situated snitches—a tax they were absolutely willing to pay to maintain their integrity and honor within the movement they risked everything for.

There wasn't a book like this available then.

In 2003, when more and more of my work became unpaid activist cases, I left the law firm where I started my career and started up my own non-profit: the Civil Liberties Defense Center (CLDC). Today, the CLDC has become nationally and globally known as a preeminent activist defense organization handling state and federal criminal activist cases, SLAPP suit defense, grand jury resistance, and federal civil rights cases against cops and feds who violate the rights of lefty activists.[4] But *the* most important asset my organization has maintained over the years is the trust we have built with activists—to fight hard and represent them as political people.

I've learned that, as a movement lawyer, you need to know the ethical rules perfectly because you will be held to a higher standard than any other lawyer. Your briefs need to be perfect. You need to think "outside the box" and be creative in your motion practice. I was told more than once by a mentor that if you want to argue or file a motion that doesn't exist, you have to make it up, brief it, cite to as much case-law as you can muster, and get ready to suit up and stand before the court with as much confidence and courtroom professionalism as the old white guys standing behind the prosecution's table. If you can fight like hell for your client while maintaining integrity, solidarity, and legitimacy as a lawyer, winning and losing becomes more of a spectrum than a cut-and-dried outcome.

Representing Radicals provides articulate explanation and guidance on how to be a movement lawyer as we move into an era of increasing radicalization in the face of pandemics and economic and ecological crises. We need not ask why our comrades and clients would rather go to jail than snitch, or pay restitution to the corporations they are fighting against, or why they would rather have extra jail time than apologize to a judge for their acts of economic disruption.

As of this writing, I have been a movement lawyer for twenty-three years—half my life! I have represented over

4,500 activists for free, mentored over seventy law students and new lawyers, and conducted over 1,000 Know Your Rights trainings for activists (who was counting?). This publication is essential to ensure that the lessons learned, the victories achieved, and the losses suffered are shared to make the movement lawyers of the future stronger, better, and faster.

With the existential threat of catastrophic climate change within the next decade, the next generation will not have decades to learn the tricks of the trade. We must have each other's backs and work cooperatively to defend our people and each other. As State repression continues to ratchet down upon humanity, radical lawyering must increase. We cannot expect a fair fight, but fight we must—with everything we've got. I hope to see you on the front lines and in the courtroom!

Lauren Regan
December 6, 2020
Eugene, Oregon

Introduction

The goal of this book is to help you understand and work well with your radical clients, particularly when they are facing criminal charges due to political repression and are approaching their case from a **movement perspective**. To achieve this goal, we are guided by our belief that attorneys and their radical clients can work together collaboratively in shared struggle when dealing with criminal charges. We believe that our struggles for **liberation** require creativity, dedication, and the willingness to rebel from lawyers, radical defendants, **legal workers** and supporters, and everyone else involved in social **movements**. This book is one way we have tried to put this belief and our **anarchist** principles into practice and to contribute to the many struggles for liberation that inspire us.

Terms in bold are listed in the Glossary.

Working as an attorney in **solidarity** with social movements might require new responsibilities and approaches. At times, these approaches may require creative legal strategies and collaborations with people other than your client. For example, one important part of working in solidarity with radical clients is to demystify the **criminal legal system** for them and their supporters while helping your client understand the realities of their situation and the limitations of what may be legally possible. Additionally, you may help your client set and pursue their legal goals within the confines of the criminal legal system while supporting their efforts to achieve their personal and political goals. You might also help support a media strategy devised by your client and/or their defense committee while maintaining your attention primarily on the legal strategy. Whatever this approach requires of you with respect to your client, it can be helpful to consider it an act of solidarity with your client and their social movements.

We also hope that this book will be useful for any attorney interested in client-centered litigation, as the quality of representation we advocate for is by no means intended to only be for people who pass a political "litmus test." None of our ideas or arguments are meant to exceptionalize the types of clients we are talking about in this book, but rather they are meant to highlight the unique needs of a distinct type of client whose decisions about their criminal charges are informed by their desire to resist **systemic oppression**. This book also does not attempt to tell you how to be a lawyer or how to litigate, nor are the ideas here intended to be construed as legal advice or continuing legal education.

We strongly believe that all prosecutions are political, and indeed that the criminal legal system and

prison-industrial complex themselves are inherently re-pressive systems rather than being societal mechanisms for ensuring justice. In tangible terms, this is seen in the dispro-portionate rates of arrests, prosecutions, convictions, and incarceration of oppressed communities, particularly poor, Black, Brown, Indigenous, **queer**, **transgender**, and un-documented ones. Laws are written by those in power and are meant to protect their interests and values. For example, over half of the 2.3 million people incarcerated pretrial and postconviction in the United States are held for nonvio-lent offenses, whereas systemic violence such as evictions and gentrification, racially biased housing and education, stop-and-frisk policing, et cetera, are supported by myriad governmental institutions and economic policies.[1] When people seek to challenge these oppressive systems, we can understand the criminal charges against them as "political" or "politically motivated." However, we do not mean that these charges are "less criminal" than other charges, that charges against activists are "more political" than charges against other people, or that activists deserve better repre-sentation than other defendants.

We authored this book and our first book, a guide for radical defendants, as companion pieces. In 2017, we pub-lished our first book, *A Tilted Guide to Being a Defendant*.[2] This book was the result of a years-long effort to distill much of what we had learned over more than a decade of defendant/**prisoner** support into a reader-friendly for-mat; it aims to be a resource for people involved in radi-cal struggles and to assist them in navigating their criminal charges. In that book, we provide a three-part framework for defendants who are figuring out how to set and balance their **legal goals**, **personal goals**, and/or **political goals** when facing criminal charges. Since its publication, we've seen it used as a resource for hundreds of people across the country facing criminal charges stemming from their political activity; and have received a lot of positive feedback about its usefulness. We hope that, in combination, these books can help attorneys, radical clients, and their **comrades** and supporters work collaboratively in shared struggle.

This book is written for attorneys with a variety of professional experiences—attorneys who find the radical political context new or confusing, politically aligned attorneys (often called **movement attorneys**), law students, and more. We understand that many attorneys will be familiar with representing radical clients, many will have been involved in radical social struggles (perhaps even facing criminal charges of their own) before becoming attorneys, and many will be new to this particular type of lawyering. We hope to give everyone useful thoughts on how to work most effectively with your radical clients, and that our ideas around client-centered lawyering may be useful in your work with *all* **people facing charges**.

We begin this guide by sharing thoughts on what representing radical clients can entail and why this is important (chapter 1). We then describe common scenarios you may face while working with radical clients (chapter 2), provide suggestions on ways to work in collaboration with your clients in shared struggle (chapter 3), and describe what political support for radicals often looks like and how this can be beneficial for everyone (chapter 4). We end the book with thoughts on working with several types of media during **political prosecutions** (chapter 5). To help provide context, we have also included a glossary.

We hope that the ideas you find here are useful. Our aim is to transform the process of fighting criminal charges into something that can strengthen and embolden our social movements rather than weakening them. As an attorney, you can play a key role in this struggle by working in solidarity with your clients.

Chapter 1: Representing Radical Clients

Chapter Outline

1.0 Defending Radical Clients

Defending a radical client facing criminal charges connected to political activity or associations may be different from other cases you've handled. The challenges that surface might seem to run counter to how you've been trained to represent your clients. Throughout this book, we encourage you to embrace these challenges when doing so can lead to a more robust defense for your individual client and their political movements. This is not meant to downplay or override your ethical and professional training and requirements, but rather to advocate for creative understandings of how those obligations can be met while supporting liberatory political movements.

1.1 What Do We Mean by "Radical"?

We use the terms "radical defendant" or "radical client" as umbrella terms for a wide variety of people.[1] We acknowledge that the term is imperfect and may not define everyone whose attorney could benefit from reading this book. By "radical," we mean that the person takes militant or revolutionary action that opposes the government, capitalism, and/or systemic oppression. Their criminal charges can be understood as a governmental response to radical actions, associations, and/or ideologies—in short, repression. Such people may identify as anarchists, communists, socialists, radicals, leftists, post-left, part of social struggle, or otherwise. But by no means do we restrict this term to only mean people who participate in political activity considered to be "activism" or "social struggle" to the exclusion of people who confront the brutalities of the criminal legal system and prison-industrial complex in their daily lives and seek to change, overhaul, or overthrow these systems. That is, we are not focusing on activists to the exclusion of people who don't identify as such but who understand their situations in political terms.

The term "radical client" also includes people who may not hold "radical" beliefs or whose charges may not fit within the confines of "protesting" but whose cases highlight the need for larger societal transformation. One example is defendants who faced rioting charges following the Ferguson uprising in 2014. Widespread social unrest—during which many stores were vandalized, burned, and looted, and projectiles were thrown at police—began after the police murdered local Black teenager, Mike Brown, on August 9, 2014. The uprising continued into November of that year when Brown's killer, police officer Darren Wilson, was not indicted on criminal charges. The uprising spread nationally, and demonstrators—many of whom were Black residents of poor and segregated neighborhoods—were arrested and charged with rioting. Although not every person arrested may have held radical political beliefs or values, their charges can be understood as part of a larger political narrative of crackdowns on multifaceted rebellion against police, prisons, racism, and the government. Many of those facing charges (and their supporters) have spoken and written publicly about their perspectives on this brutal police killing and its aftermath, highlighting the implications for **social justice** and the liberation of oppressed communities, particularly poor Black ones.

An unfortunate limitation of this book is that "radical client" and "movement attorney" do not necessarily include people embroiled in either the criminal legal or civil legal systems who are seeking to change society for the better by fighting the systems from within, such as social workers or public defenders. Many people slog through long legal battles of all sorts to address systemic oppression in governmental and nongovernmental institutions and policies, police and other governmental targeting of historically oppressed and marginalized communities, and economic policies that destroy communities and ecosystems, to name just a few broad areas. People who fight these fights often do so because of fervent desires to address social injustices. Although there will hopefully be useful ideas in this book for people taking on those roles, this book likely will not address their needs and priorities sufficiently.

1.2 Important Roles for Attorneys Representing Radicals

There are many important roles for attorneys who are working as part of or in solidarity with movements for social justice and liberation—too many for this guide to delve into. Moreover, there are many radical and legal organizations working hard every day to leverage the benefits and privileges that can come with a law degree. We have a list of resources available on our website (tiltedscalescollective.org); the National Lawyers Guild (NLG) bears specific mentioning here, as it is a progressive organization of lawyers, law students, legal workers, and **jailhouse lawyers** that works in solidarity with radical social movements, as well as Law for Black Lives (L4BL).

Many lawyers dedicate their careers to fighting for social justice through the courts or take on political cases in addition to their full-time jobs. This work has clearly benefited many individuals and communities in direct, tangible ways, as well as society in a broader sense in less quantifiable ways. If your motivations and aspirations as an attorney fall into this realm, representing radicals will undoubtedly fit in well with your political goals. If you are sympathetic to your client's goals and aspirations, you will likely find that your representation presents opportunities to contribute to social movements in concrete ways while fulfilling your obligations as the attorney.

Another important role that many lawyers can play is strategizing ways of using the criminal and/or civil legal system to advance struggles for social justice and liberation. The myriad opportunities for lawyering in these ways are outside the scope of this book, but many lawyers and organizations dedicate themselves to fighting these fights. As mentioned previously, we briefly describe many of these organizations in the resource list available on our website.

1.3 Political Prosecutions

The treatment of defendants in political prosecutions may seem unusually aggressive compared to cases with similar charges, both in tone and tactics used. Prosecutors may pull tricks that differ from routine court practice, even if they don't technically break the rules. Common examples include prosecutors pushing for unusually high bail/bond amounts (or no bail), filing superseding indictments on the eve of (or immediately after) court appearances to shake up the defense, withholding evidence, using the media to vilify the defendant, or seeking to admit First Amendment materials as evidence (e.g., books, clothing with political slogans, et cetera). These prosecutorial abuses are by no means unique to prosecutions against radicals, but they are frequently part of these cases. In mentioning this feature of political prosecutions, we don't mean to downplay the horrific violence courts enact daily upon all people ensnared in the legal system, but to elucidate how prosecutions against radicals may differ from typical prosecutions.

Although these tactics used by the prosecution are clearly motivated by the politics of the case, both the judge and prosecutor will most likely deny every attempt *by the defense* to address these motivations. This can be especially frustrating if your client has been targeted by an informant or has been entrapped by undercover agents—both of which almost always involve the government targeting radical movements under the guise of focusing on criminalized activity. In prosecutions against radicals, the government will do everything in its power to control the

Punished for Political Action: The Case of Ramsey Orta
by Andrew Plasse, Esq.

In 2014, Ramsey Orta filmed a video on his cell phone of New York Police Department (NYPD) officer Daniel Pantaleo using a prohibited and fatal chokehold on Ramsey's friend, Eric Garner, who had been detained for allegedly selling untaxed cigarettes. Ramsey's video exposed police violence and anti-Black racism, and helped catalyze a widespread movement against systemic racism in the criminal legal system. Following Eric's death and the resulting national outcry, Ramsey was continually followed and harassed by the NYPD. In 2015, he was arrested on trumped-up drugs and weapons charges. The charges and media slander against him were retaliation used to publicly discredit his video.

His time in prison has not been easy—he's been constantly ticketed for petty or falsified offenses and has been punished for longer than other inmates in similar circumstances. The New York state parole board ensured he had enough infractions to be denied his first parole opportunity and serve the maximum time on his sentence. Ramsey also asserts that his food has been poisoned and that guards have called him racial epithets and told him to commit suicide. Ramsey's story demonstrates how the criminal legal system targets those who take public action against systemic oppression. Ramsey's case, like that of Eric Garner's, also highlights how police interactions are exponentially more harmful for people of color, especially Black men. As Ramsey pointed out, he is the only one to serve time for the death of Eric Garner.

narrative about your client, even when it means not playing by its own rules.

All that said, there are also times when prosecutions against radical defendants, the ways they're treated in court, the sentences they receive, and the repression they face when serving their sentences is markedly better than what most defendants face, particularly when those defendants are poor, people of color, and/or frequently embroiled in the criminal legal system (as are most of the people in prison and on probation in the United States). Within a

Systemic Racism and Sentencing: Josh Williams and Ferguson
by Nick Zotos, Esq.

Josh Williams was a well-known, vocal participant in the Ferguson uprising that followed the police murder of eighteen-year-old Mike Brown in 2014. He was quickly enmeshed in the resistance happening there and responded to the urgency of the historical moment, saying, "The government is not hearing us until we do something—until we make them hear us."

During Josh's time in Ferguson, police shot and killed another Black man, Antonio Martin. Josh was arrested in connection with rioting and looting that occurred in the days that followed. He was eighteen years of age and had no prior arrest record. In December 2015, Josh pleaded guilty to felony charges of arson and burglary connected to items from the gas station: a lighter, a pack of gum, and some money. He was sentenced to eight years in state prison.

Josh's harsh sentence can be understood as the government's attempt to make an example of him and to dissuade other young Black men from taking direct action. Political prosecution in this case is about compounding factors—Josh's race, militant tactics, and public visibility as a person committed to social struggle. As Josh's attorney, I made the following remarks after his sentencing: "I think Josh wound up paying a price for a lot of things going on in Ferguson that he was not responsible for. He did attempt to light a fire, but his sentence is completely disproportionate to the conduct."

group of radicals, systemic racism, classism, sexism, and other forms of oppression can work to repress certain defendants more harshly than others. These disparities can be seen by contrasting prosecutions against radicals with typical prosecutions in a jurisdiction, and how radical defendants who are people of color, transgender people, **gender-nonconforming** or **genderqueer** people, immigrants, and/or people with disabilities are often treated more poorly or receive harsher punishments than radical defendants with more social privilege.

1.4 Radical Clients Can Differ From Typical Clients

Many radical defendants find themselves in need of a lawyer after taking actions that they are aware may subject them to criminal charges. This might mean attending a protest or spontaneous gathering after a tragedy such as the police shooting someone; other times, it might mean acting intentionally to physically resist oppression (blockading Immigration and Customs Enforcement [ICE] vehicles trying to transport immigrants for deportation) or to sabotage operations that will harm the environment or communities (destroying pipeline construction equipment). No matter how your client found their way to you, odds are they already have a set of deeply held beliefs and principles—many of which are directly relevant to the criminal legal system—that may cause them to interact with you and the court process differently than your clients typically do.[2] Although radical clients may not wish to assist with case preparation at all, some may be knowledgeable about and/ or interested in participating in their own **legal defense** strategy. They may want to assist with tasks such as case law research, discovery review, investigation, and legal strategy. They may have helpful knowledge of similar cases, or access to lawyers who might be able to help you with sticky legal or political scenarios. Their experience and knowledge may be one of your strongest assets when fighting alongside them in the courtroom.

Your radical client's strongly held principles may influence how they would like their case handled. For example, they may want you to think about their defense from a **collective** or movement perspective rather than in the individualistic terms that are often mandated by the criminal legal system, even if doing so means a greater likelihood of conviction. This might require crafting a defense that doesn't distinguish them from their codefendants in ways that could be damaging to their codefendants. If the charges are about property destruction, for example, they might refuse any defense that makes them look like a "good" protester who didn't do anything wrong, unlike the "bad" protesters who broke the law, because such arguments strengthen the government's divide and conquer tactics. A collective perspective may also mean considering the personal goals and needs of more vulnerable codefendants and/or considering the impact of your client's case on their political movements more broadly. These considerations may require a defense that does not imply that someone else (whether charged as a codefendant or not) committed the offense. The nuances of this distinction are slightly rhetorical, but the important political implications are about whether or not the arguments being made in defense of one radical defendant are at the expense of others.

Creating a legal strategy for a client taking this position does not mean neglecting to provide them with a vigorous defense. Rather, it means viewing all their goals and priorities from a holistic perspective and figuring out how to best help them while effectively performing your role.

1.5 Political Support for Radical Clients

Often, **defense committees** will form for radical clients to enact political support (see chapter 4). A defense committee is a group of people—friends, family, community organizers—who provide personal support and solidarity organizing for defendants. They are called defense committees, support committees, support crews; or they could be organized as autonomous organizations, often called **legal collectives**, antirepression committees, or antirepression crews. We refer to any political formation along these lines as "defense committees" for the sake of expediency.

Defense committees can take many forms and serve many roles. Often, they provide direct support to people facing charges, fundraise to cover personal and legal expenses, and organize a political/media campaign around their case. If you are representing a client with a defense committee, you may be asked to be accountable and responsive to that group as well as to your client, even though you only have an attorney-client relationship with your client. It may be challenging to figure out how to provide your client with the high-quality defense you want to provide while also working with their defense committee to help them achieve their personal and political goals. A defense committee can serve as a crucial bridge in that regard, taking on the community organizing and direct support roles that radicals often want, but attorneys cannot perform. We further explore ways to work with defense committees to support clients in chapter 4.

1.6 Political Defenses

The decision to mount a **political defense** should come from considering your client's legal, personal, and political goals in relationship to the political movements of which they are a part. Political defenses can mean adding in political statements to opening and closing arguments; infusing the political points a client wants to make in all aspects of the trial (voir dire, cross-examination, testimony, et cetera), even at the risk of running afoul of the rules of procedure or court orders; refusing to participate in the trial proceedings or challenging the legitimacy of the court's authority; or any combination of these, or something entirely different that a client and their political movements may desire. Your client and their comrades may wish to mount a political defense for several reasons, including to:

- Use their case to build support for and draw attention to their cause, while exposing the politics of the case or the nature of the political persecution (necessity defense and antipipeline organizing);

- Challenge the use of charges that may set a potentially damaging precedent if there were a conviction (conspiracy charges, rioting charges, et cetera);

- Publicly expose or pressure a prosecutor and/or other politicians (mayor, governor) who align themselves with a successful prosecution;

- Reject the legitimacy of the government to press charges, enact punishments, incarcerate people, or exert control of the territory the government claims to have sovereignty over; or

- Speak the moral, political, ethical, religious, or spiritual truth that the defendant believes is more important than whatever consequences they may face because of doing so.

Often, a political defense involves some level of legal risk, including conviction and/or contempt of court. Attorneys representing radicals may have difficulty understanding why their clients desire political defenses, especially when these potentially come at the expense of their legal defenses. Others may see their roles as attorneys as positioning them to help their clients achieve their personal and political goals through a political defense, or a combination of a political and legal defense, even when doing so has entailed risks to the attorneys (e.g., contempt of court or other censure from the judge). Numerous political struggles, from Black liberation movements to antipipeline movements, have circumvented serious legal repression and/or achieved significant political gains by partnering with lawyers to find creative legal approaches to robust representation.

2.0 A Movement Perspective

Looking at a case from a movement perspective means that your client is likely to maintain a strong commitment to noncooperation with the government. This undoubtedly includes not providing the government with any information about other people, groups, organizations, or movements. This may also mean rejecting deals offered by the prosecution if they include provisions that will hurt others or social movements. Examples of undesirable plea agreements could be agreements that require the defendant to provide information on others, refer to others' actions in the statement of facts, or include provisions that will hamper a movement's ability to protest and participate in political organizing. Although this may feel frustrating to you if you are not used to working with people whose principles dictate a strong "no **snitching**" mindset and movement perspective, these are often top concerns for radical clients.

2.1 Political Pressure Campaigns

Your client's case may also be the subject of a broad **political pressure campaign**, and so there may be media created, petitions circulated, letter-writing nights organized, and protests against the prosecutor to drop the charges. These efforts typically run simultaneously with the legal proceedings, remaining separate from them but having many interlinkages and overlaps (in timing, content of messaging, et cetera). They also often use a client's situation to highlight broader systemic oppression. This type of activity outside of the courtroom may seem to pose potential friction or even harm to the legal strategy, but political pressure campaigns can have powerful results and are commonly used in political cases. For example, they can allow for dialogue and create sympathy within the public and the media in ways that can dramatically affect the outcome of the case in both the public mind and the courtroom.

For attorneys, these pressure campaigns may also provide opportunities to use their position to work on the issues that motivated them to pursue a career in law in the first place, or to work strategically with other lawyers to challenge unjust laws and sentencing practices.

A radical client may also desire to use the legal process itself as a political pressure campaign. For example, they may want arguments made in their defense to highlight the oppressive structures they were protesting against, including in their opening and closing arguments at trial. Or they may want to put the criminal legal system, the police, or the government on trial by using the legal process to make political statements against these institutions. Or they may reject the authority of the US government to try them at all (as some Puerto Rican independence fighters have done) and thus refuse to participate in criminal legal proceedings entirely.[3]

When radical clients approach their cases with any of these interests in mind, minimizing the harm of a conviction or achieving the best legal result for them as an individual may be less important to them than working with their codefendants, rejecting the prosecution's characterizations of them and their movements, and minimizing the damage done to radical political movements. Lawyers representing radicals need to understand their client's perspective on their charges and, often, their valuing of the movement and their comrades over their own self-interest.

2.2 Case Study of Political Prosecutions

A recent example of client values directing the course of trial strategies and media narratives about political prosecutions is the case of the defendants arrested at an **anticapitalist/antifascist** march in Washington, D.C., on January 20, 2017 in protest of Trump's inauguration. In the "J20 case," more than two hundred people were arrested and nearly all were indicted as codefendants on a felony rioting charge. Two superseding indictments were later filed that dropped some defendants from the indictment; added some previously unindicted people to the charges; and upped the blanket charges to multiple felony counts (inciting riot and property destruction) and misdemeanor counts (conspiracy to riot, engaging in a riot, resisting arrest, and assault on an officer). The arrestees were facing more than sixty years in prison if convicted and given consecutive sentences (realistically, they were facing around a decade if sentenced concurrently). Mass convictions might have created a damaging precedent for policing at other mass mobilizations in D.C. A large number of convictions might have also encouraged the government to press for conspiracy charges in the future despite a lack of individual probable cause.

Taking plea agreements to lower-level charges would have been legally sensible for many people, especially if they were not individually accused of damaging property or organizing the demonstration. Nevertheless, most of the accused agreed to "Points of Unity" that asserted they *would not* cooperate with the prosecution (including testifying or making statements against other defendants), *would* share information and resources to help each other fight their charges, and *would* support each other's individual decisions as long as they were not at anyone else's expense. Later political messaging and organizing concentrated on defendants taking their cases to trial unless all the charges were dropped for every person who was charged.

Two trials took place in this case. The first, in November 2017, ended in full acquittals for all six arrestees. Soon after, in January 2018, the prosecutor dropped charges against more than a hundred others. The next trial, in May 2018, resulted in either acquittals or a hung jury on the charges for all four radicals on trial. While this trial was happening, defense pretrial motions for upcoming trials revealed that the prosecutor had withheld exculpatory evidence from the defense; namely, videos taken by a far-right group that had surreptitiously filmed political organizing meetings in the lead-up to the inauguration. After this second failure to secure convictions at trial for even a misdemeanor charge, and with further sanctions from the court due to the discovery violation, the prosecution dropped all charges against the remaining defendants. In the end, only one person pleaded guilty to a felony charge of property destruction and served four months in prison, and less than two dozen pleaded guilty to misdemeanor charges of rioting and only served probation.

This case is an instructive example because of the unusual legal developments, which ranged from blanket charges for more than two hundred people without individualized probable cause to the prosecutor getting caught hiding evidence. Much creative and assertive litigation happened in the case as well, which led to the prosecution revealing the evidence they had been hiding. The people facing charges had political commitments to each other and to fighting the charges despite their individual "best legal option." These principles served as the foundation that allowed for all these legal developments to occur. Without this solidarity, the case would not have resulted in the overwhelmingly successful legal and political outcomes, and undoubtedly would have been resolved in the standard way: massive numbers of plea agreements, with few or no trials.

3.0 The Defendant's Goal-Setting Framework and Its Impact on Lawyering

The J20 case is also a good example of the three-part goal-setting framework for people facing charges that we presented in *A Tilted Guide to Being a Defendant*. The three areas are legal, personal, and political. Legal goals are what lawyers are trained to counsel their clients in, such as winning acquittals or dropped charges, negotiating plea agreements to lower-level charges to avoid felony convictions and prison time, or negotiating plea agreements that reduce collateral consequences. Personal goals are ones that people facing charges set to care for themselves and their loved ones, such as avoiding prison time no matter how the case resolves because they have people who are dependent on them. Political goals are ones that prioritize advancing political struggles, such as valuing solidarity and movements for liberation over the potential for suffering negative consequences, using trial to deliver political messages, or getting convicted and serving time to make a moral statement about injustice.

This framework is situated in the context of governmental repression against radicals, by which we mean criminal charges slapped on protesters (at street protests, encampments/occupations, uprisings, et cetera) and people whose actions challenge institutional power who are targeted by the cops and courts as part of daily systemic oppression. The latter might be someone who is charged with vagrancy who understands their so-called crime as a challenge to the myth of a benevolent capitalist society, or a person of color charged with assault after defending against a white supremacist attacker. Further, this framework is presented as reinforcement for two fundamental movement values: 1) we don't provide the government with information that will help them lock people in cages (i.e., we don't snitch); and 2) our criminal charges are part of our struggles for liberation and social justice.

Although there is overlap between the three goal areas, people facing charges may be interested in prioritizing other aspects of their cases above the legal ones. For example, a radical client may be more interested in using the court process to highlight the repressive nature of their charges than in pursuing a plea deal for lesser sentencing. An attorney representing radicals can help them determine their legal goals and the best legal strategy, as well as figure out how these relate to their personal and political goals. This means helping your client think through their situation and what is realistic or sensible from a legal perspective, even when it requires creative lawyering to figure out how best to support your client in ways that may be novel or unusual.

3.1 Working With Your Client on Their Goal Areas

Lawyers representing radicals should approach their representation as a collaboration with a peer in a joint endeavor. By this, we mean not only being client centered throughout trial preparation, but also working to ensure your client is supported in pursuing all their goals for their cases. Part of this entails breaking down or overcoming barriers to effective collaboration, whether these are limitations imposed by pretrial incarceration, differences in priorities and values, power differentials between lawyers and clients, or interpersonal conflicts or tensions within the attorney-client relationship. At times, approaching this type of representation may be nearly identical to most cases; other times, it may mean working quite differently. For example, a radical client who wants to be involved in creating the legal strategy and be vocal within the media about the political issues surrounding the case may require a different approach to lawyering than is typical, particularly if media attention influences the prosecutor's approach to the case.

Understanding a radical client's political goals can often be a challenging part of this approach. Much of this guide is written on this important aspect of representing radicals, and here it is important to stress how understanding your client's political goals can help you come up with less common legal options and ways to help them meet their overall goals. By understanding and prioritizing your client's personal and political goals, as well as their legal ones, you can provide higher quality representation without coming into conflict with your ethical and professional obligations. We further explore ways of approaching representation in this way in chapter 3.

4.0 Clarifying and Centering Client Goals and Strategy

Perhaps the most important part of your work with radical clients is being sure to center their goals, needs, and strategies—legal, personal, and political. Attorneys representing radical clients often need to be creative in finding ways to help them advance their political goals while navigating the criminal legal system. For example, it might be important for your client to put the politics of their case center stage, whether in the courtroom or outside of it, even if that approach carries with it the possibility of damaging their chances of a positive legal outcome. Another common scenario is where the client wants the charges to be dropped entirely, and thus the legal team works on legal strategies to accomplish this while the defense committee works on a political pressure campaign against the prosecutor to raise public awareness and to make it politically desirable for the prosecutor to let the case fade away quietly. Helping your client find ways to stay true to their values while making strategic legal decisions is an important part of representing radicals.

We recommend that people facing charges honestly assess their personal, political, and legal goals before pursuing a particular legal or political strategy. In *A Tilted Guide to Being a Defendant*, we outlined a framework for thinking through these questions when facing charges. We also advocate that radicals consult with their comrades, friends, family, and loved ones to gain perspective when making decisions about their cases—albeit without damaging attorney-client privilege. Your client should understand that discussions with you are intended to help them grasp the legal implications of pursuing various goals, strategies, and tactics over others. We recommend that attorneys take time when first meeting with their clients to understand their goals. Talking through all three goal areas will likely be a dynamic process, as attorneys often have insights into the legal aspects of the case that help clients make educated decisions about their legal goals. Likewise, lawyers will generally benefit from learning more about their clients' other priorities and desires (i.e., personal and political) for their cases. Having open conversations about goals and priorities early on can help both of you identify ways in which your ideas and expectations about the case may differ, be in conflict with each other, or create complications for each other.

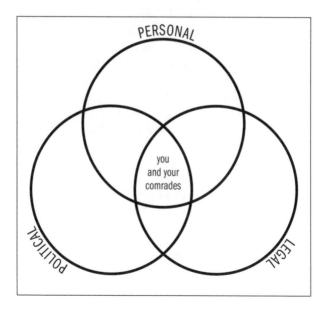

4.1 Jointly Setting Legal Goals

As with any client, radical people facing criminal charges often benefit from frank discussions about the statutory consequences they face, what is realistic for their particular jurisdiction and judge, and what sentence might be likely based on their criminal history or any mitigating factors. Many times, however, radical clients might have different priorities than typical defendants, such as preferring executed sentences that just require jail time but no supervised release or probation, or preferring more jail time over paying restitution. Pushing for the legal outcome that your client desires may be an important part of helping them develop realistic expectations and pursue legal goals that they can live with.

It's also possible that your client may be surprised by the severity of the potential consequences they are facing. If your client has a rude awakening about the risks associated with conviction, you may find that your typical responsibilities as a lawyer to explain the potential outcomes to your client have the additional component of discussing how these realities affect your client's overall goals for their case.

Further, it's possible that you might disagree with your client's legal goals, consider them to not be in their best interests, or simply think that they are misguided or naïve. Many lawyers representing radical clients have struggled to understand their legal goals, so you are not alone if this is true for you. Nevertheless, representing radical clients may require you to push yourself to understand their goals and priorities, as well as to explain to them the potential legal outcomes.

4.2 Guiding Questions for Balancing Goal Areas

In this subsection, we offer questions to help you talk with your client about their legal, personal, and political goals. These are meant to be examples and starting points rather than a question-by-question guide, but we hope that they help facilitate effective conversations. As we discuss at length in *A Tilted Guide to Being a Defendant*, these goal areas are highly interrelated, as well as somewhat arbitrary, so the following is meant to aid discussion rather than to impose strict categories for understanding the myriad of questions, considerations, and potential consequences that accompany criminal charges.

4.2.1 Legal Goals

- Is getting the charges thrown out the primary concern? Is this important to your client so that they can get the arrest and charges expunged from their record? Is it important to prevent (or at least delay) the government from securing a conviction under a new law?

- Is acquittal at trial the primary concern? Would an acquittal boost your client's movement? In contrast, would a conviction hurt it substantially?

- Is taking the case to trial, regardless of the likelihood of prevailing or of the potential consequences, the most important consideration?

- Is testifying at trial an important goal (personal or political) for your client, and thus is pushing through to trial important?

- Are there possibly damaging legal precedents that could come out of a conviction? Is taking the case to trial important for trying to set a beneficial precedent?

- Is this precedent a legal one, such as a trial court ruling that may have a strong chance of being upheld by an appeals court or, ultimately, the state and/or federal Supreme Courts?

- Is it a political one, such as showing other radicals across the country that it's worth fighting back?

- How much do your client's legal goals align with the goals of their codefendants in this case? Are there conflicting or competing areas that need to be addressed to figure out your client's own legal goals?

- How much do your client's legal goals align with the legal goals of other radical people and groups across the country who have faced the same or similar charges?

4.2.2 Personal Goals

- How will the arrest record or a conviction affect your client's ability to secure housing, employment, student loans, professional licensing, et cetera? What is your client willing to deal with because of facing these charges or a conviction?

- How would a conviction affect your client's parental rights or status as a caregiver for someone who is dependent on them? What other legal representation may they need to address all these considerations (e.g., wills, power of attorney or medical power of attorney, child support, et cetera)?

- How will an arrest record or a conviction affect a client who is petitioning for asylum, permanent residency, or citizenship?

- How would short or long-term incarceration affect your client's health? Do they need access to medications of any kind, or expect that they might need access over the long term?

- How would short or long-term incarceration affect your client's gender expression and identity? Do they need access to healthcare providers who are experienced with transgender/gender-nonconforming patients? Do they need access to gender-affirming medications and procedures (e.g., medications such as exogenous hormones and androgen-blockers, or procedures such as electrolysis or surgery)?

• Would an extended pretrial process or lengthy trial adversely affect your client's mental health? Or would any length of incarceration, particularly a long sentence, be problematic? Is their life in danger because of these charges?

4.2.3 Political Goals

• How does your client want this case to affect the movement(s) of which they are a part? Are they willing to risk a chilling effect on future protests? Alternatively, do they want to figure out ways of combating the chilling effect that is often a part of criminal charges against radicals, even if that means they might face harsher consequences themselves?

• Does your client want to use anything that can be exposed as a result of the legal proceedings in this criminal case to combat the operations of the government, the military, corporations, et cetera? This could be in terms of discovery requests, legal rulings in this particular case, rulings that may come from appeals, litigation that may result from Freedom of Information Act (FOIA) or Privacy Act requests in the future, et cetera.

- Would going through trial (or at least a sizable portion of pretrial proceedings) expose enough information about government infiltration/infiltrators/spying to provide radical organizations and movements with useful information to prepare for future state repression?

- Would beating the charges (having them thrown out pretrial, getting an acquittal at trial) signal a symbolic victory for their movements and have the potential of deterring similar state repression in the future?

- Would fighting the charges through a political defense, or a combination of legal defense and political defense, create the opportunities to ruin the careers of the prosecutor and/or other politicians who align themselves with a successful prosecution (e.g., the mayor, the governor, et cetera)? Could defeating these politicians provide political victories that are worth the risks involved?

- Would a judge or jury trial create opportunities for positive publicity for your client's movement(s), such as ones that could be created through a media strategy accompanying their legal and political strategies? Could the charges and/or your client as a person generate public sympathy for their cause in a courtroom, even if they are convicted?

- Does your client believe they could do more good for their movement(s) outside of prison or inside? Do they see any benefits or drawbacks of their potential incarceration on a *political* level?

4.3 When Goals Conflict

Radical people facing charges sometimes find that their goal areas conflict and that tradeoffs become necessary. Oftentimes, this is because the criminal legal system is brutally effective at forcing people into no-win situations that only give the choice between a bad outcome and a worse one, if any choice at all. Conflicts can also arise when defendants want to achieve multiple goals that are incompatible under the circumstances, such as not cooperating against others and not going to prison when the prosecution is only willing to offer a plea agreement that involves cooperation and going to trial has a high risk of conviction and incarceration.

When these conflicts arise, your usual role of advising your clients on their options and the potential consequences of their legal decisions may entail discussing their personal and political goals as well. You may not want to offer thoughts on these other goal areas, or your client may not want your advice on these areas. Nevertheless, having clear understandings of what are *legal* goals, *legal* decisions, and *legal* consequences can help both of you sort through the intricacies of these tough decisions. This clear understanding can also help you understand all of your client's priorities so you can be assured that their decisions are well informed, even if they ultimately make decisions that you don't consider to be in their best legal interests.

Additionally, it is not uncommon for attorney and client goals to conflict. This can be true whether the attorney has opinions about political decisions in the case or not, as well as when the attorney has opinions about the legal significance of the case. For example, an attorney may want to take a case to trial because it seems to have a high chance of

---

Beyond Legal Goals: The Fred Hampton Case
by Jeffrey Haas, Esq., cofounder of the People's Law Office (PLO)

On December 4, 1969, under the direction of Cook County state attorney Edward Hanrahan, the Chicago police shot up Black Panther chairperson Fred Hampton's apartment and murdered him and Mark Clark, another prominent Panther leader. The raid was meant to "neutralize" Panther influence in Chicago and involved collaboration with the FBI. I was part of a team of movement attorneys who represented the seven Panther survivors, who were indicted on charges of attempted murder, armed violence, and other weapons charges.

In my book on the assassination, I write:

"We were faced with the seeming contradiction between the need to tell the public what happened, and thus provide support for the growing tide of opposition to Hanrahan or, alternatively, to provide what some considered the best legal defense for the survivors. Our group decision was to take the offensive, to tell the press what happened as recounted by the survivors and as demonstrated by the physical evidence.... We presented the case in a political, not a criminal framework.... We learned it was the best strategy to expose government wrongdoing and educate the public and to put the state on trial. It was also the best strategy to win."*

* Jeffrey Haas, *The Assassination of Fred Hampton: How the FBI and the Chicago Police Murdered a Black Panther* (Chicago: Lawrence Hill Press, 2019).

a positive verdict that would be upheld on appeal and strike a blow against an unjust law, but the client wants to resolve the case quickly and not jeopardize their ability to care for dependents in their life. Or the client might want to take the case to trial no matter what, even though the attorney may not want to risk losing and seeing their client locked up. There is no rubric to create a perfect, harm-free plan, and the client has the final say on what they do with their case. Despite the lack of perfect solutions, there are ways for radical clients to make sound decisions in consultation with their attorneys that preserve their due process rights, center their goals and needs, and satisfy the attorney's need to provide them with a robust defense.

4.4 Adapting Goals

Cases change over time; thus, it is important to consider how legal, personal, and political goals may evolve over time. Attorneys, their clients, and defense committees having timely check-in conversations about all the goal areas, any tensions or conflicts among them, and the client's priorities as the case changes can be a good way of ensuring that the client is well supported for making decisions about their case.

Chapter 2: Common Situations in Cases Against Radicals

Chapter Outline

1.0 Introduction

There are some commonalities in the kinds of repression radical clients face, the charges brought against them, their available defenses, and how they proceed given all these factors. These commonalities are in part a result of the values shared by many radicals, and often a result of the vehemence with which their cases are pursued by the prosecution. This chapter lays out common situations in cases against radicals, as well as defenses and other legal maneuvers that radical clients often choose. These choices are often based on both the legal goals and strategies they decide on with their attorneys and their own personal and political goals. As mentioned previously, this can be part of a client-centered approach to working with any client, even if the goal areas in our framework are not the ones any particular client would choose for themself.

Rather than doing an exhaustive examination of the various mechanisms that can be used in each jurisdiction, we focus on how they are often used in repression of radicals and movements. Likewise, rather than trying to predict what your individual clients might want to pursue in their cases, we examine approaches that are common among radical clients that may be unfamiliar to many attorneys.

2.0 Mechanisms of Political Repression

This section outlines many of the common mechanisms of political repression used against radical defendants and provides tools for best defending against them. One reason your client may have been targeted is that the government may believe they know something of value, or that they are a visible and/or outspoken part of their community and struggle; tying them up with charges and/or incarcerating them may significantly stall, disrupt, or ruin their organizing efforts. These clients may also have been the subject of surveillance that might eventually lead to Brady violations, which can work in a defendant's favor.[1]

Throughout the last several decades, movements for Indigenous, Black, Puerto Rican, and Latinx liberation, and other political struggles led by people of color, have

Exposing Digital Surveillance
by the Electronic Frontier Foundation (EFF)

Always try to understand how law enforcement identified your client. Figuring out how your client ended up in law enforcement's crosshairs might be easy (e.g., your client is arrested during a protest). But if your client participated in a protest and then was arrested days later, the methods police used to find your client may be more opaque.

Often, law enforcement relies on some type of digital surveillance before making an arrest, such as reviewing publicly available social media posts, obtaining private messages from companies like Facebook or Twitter, or getting real-time location information from a phone provider.

This surveillance often relies on untested legal theories in an area of the law that is constantly in flux. Depending on the type of surveillance and the type of legal process used, challenging these surveillance methods can often be a productive avenue for suppressing evidence—especially when there is a heightened First Amendment concern arising from the investigation.

been subject to extreme repression in the form of surveillance, infiltration, police violence, extrajudicial murders, and extremely long prison sentences. Examples include the Black Panther Party and Black Liberation Army, the American Indian Movement, the Puerto Rican independence struggle, the Ferguson and Baltimore uprisings, Palestine solidarity organizations, Black Lives Matter, and water protectors at Standing Rock, among others. A well-documented campaign of this repression is COIN-TELPRO ("Counterintelligence Program"), which officially ran from 1956 to 1971 before it was publicly exposed and (officially) shut down. During this time, the FBI ran a covert campaign against domestic political groups, aiming to "expose, disrupt, misdirect, or otherwise neutralize the activities of black-nationalist, hate-type organisations and groupings, their leadership, spokesmen, membership and supporters."[2] The long history of political repression against communities of color, in conjunction with systemic oppression of these communities, is a painful reminder that people of color are always at risk of harsher punishment when targeted by the government.

2.1 Government Infiltration

One of the most common tactics used in state repression is infiltration. The government often relies on informants, undercovers, and plainclothes cops to gather intelligence on radical movements, groups, and individuals. These informants could operate undercover for years before their existence is known to anyone they are targeting. Their reach into movements can be long and highly damaging. Their notes, recordings, and debriefs are often an indispensable part of prosecutions. Their recollections of the alleged statements or actions of your client may be used extensively with no other corroboration.

A common function of infiltrators is to entrap people in conspiracies and push them to take concrete actions that can be the basis of prosecutions. The presence of informants and undercovers doesn't necessarily mean that radicals have been entrapped, however. These agents can serve many functions, including *agents provocateur*, *agents suppressant*, or simple intelligence gatherers.

If an informant has been involved in your client's case, they might be experiencing an added component of emotional fallout from their arrest. The normal fear,

Uncovering Infiltration and Movement Surveillance
by Molly Armour, Esq.

Uncovering infiltration and movement surveillance can be a tough legal challenge, especially when a corporate interest engages private security, such as we saw at Standing Rock. Constitutional protections typically extend only to government actors, making unregulated actions of private security difficult to expose and challenge, even while they funnel information to and act as an extension of law enforcement. But, strong evidence of coordination between private security and the government may help movements defeat claims that such actions and information are shielded from disclosure.

Additionally, understanding which law enforcement agencies are on the ground, their mandates and joint agreements, what information is shared with them (e.g., security briefings) and what information they collect (e.g., video surveillance, body cameras) can be essential to gathering all material and/or exculpatory information.

Organized and comprehensive review of large volumes of information is vital. Time, energy, and resources are important in tackling voluminous information. In defense of Red Fawn Fallis, our legal team drew from vast volumes of media, photographs, and video that were expertly gathered, catalogued, and reviewed by the Water Protector Legal Collective.

It is essential to make early, specific, written requests to the government and to educate judges on why disclosure should be ordered. Courts are rarely sympathetic to political clients, so be prepared to shoehorn requests into standard criminal buckets—discovery rules, evidence of bias and motive, Brady material, et cetera.

anxiety, dread, and uncertainty that come along with an arrest may be compounded by feelings of the most awful betrayal. They may feel like there is no one they can trust (including any codefendants). Your client may be experiencing post-traumatic stress as a result of their experiences; there are increasingly sophisticated resources about using a **trauma-informed framework** when working with traumatized people that would be useful for any criminal defense attorney. They will likely need to know that they can trust you to do what you say you will do. It might also be beneficial for you to help them rebuild or maintain trust and collaboration with their codefendants and their codefendants' counsel. The government routinely uses lack of trust to pressure people facing charges to turn against one another.

When an informant has also acted as an *agent provocateur*, it might be useful to consider examining the potential for an entrapment defense (see Section 5.1 in this chapter). Informants and *agents provocateur* are nothing new in radical movements or in other campaigns of state repression, such as the so-called War on Terror. Their use has been well documented and researched.[3] Two case studies can help illustrate the devastating effects of entrapment: the cases of Eric McDavid and Red Fawn Fallis.

McDavid was arrested in January 2006 and charged with conspiracy to commit arson, allegedly as a member of the Earth Liberation Front (ELF). Soon after his arrest, McDavid and his comrades realized that they had been associating with an FBI informant for the previous year and a half. "Anna" was someone they considered a friend, and she had spent the entirety of that time drawing McDavid in romantically and creating a "conspiracy." At the time of the arrest, the group was living in a cabin paid for by Anna (i.e., by the FBI) that was completely wired with audio/video surveillance. McDavid took his case to trial and, although the group never attempted to carry out any actions, he was convicted and sentenced to almost twenty years in prison. After his trial, several jurors went on record saying they were embarrassed by the FBI's actions and, although there was clear evidence of entrapment, they felt hamstrung by the jury instructions and believed they had to convict.[4] Almost a decade into his sentence, McDavid's habeas corpus petition gained traction with a Brady violation; he was able to negotiate a plea agreement to a lesser included charge after a FOIA request revealed that the FBI had withheld evidence of Anna's communications with him that suggested romantic interest. This resolution allowed him to walk free half-way through his sentence.

Fallis is an Oglala Lakota woman who played an influential role as a water protector at the Standing Rock encampment in North Dakota. She became the subject of an FBI operation that, as part of a multifaceted campaign of state repression against water protectors, sought to disrupt and discredit opponents of the Dakota Access Pipeline (DAPL). On October 27, 2016, after an altercation between police and water protectors in which three gunshots were allegedly fired, Fallis was arrested and charged with civil disorder, possession of a firearm and ammunition by a convicted felon, and discharge of a firearm in relation to a felony crime of violence. The legal owner of the gun

Fallis was alleged to have fired was a paid FBI informant named Heath Harmon, who had become Fallis's boyfriend after infiltrating the encampment. Her lawyers challenged her charges on constitutional grounds, saying she was seized without probable cause while engaging in protected speech. In January 2018, Fallis accepted a **noncooperating plea agreement** for the first two charges in exchange for a dismissal of the discharge of a firearm in relation to a felony crime of violence charge, which carried a minimum sentence of ten years and the potential of life in prison. She was released in September 2020.

2.2 Cooperative Witnesses

Cops and prosecutors use cooperative witnesses to gain information they did not know beforehand and to gain leverage over those witnesses, the people they want to target for charges, and movements as a whole. It is also true that antiauthoritarian and leftist communities generally have strong values against cooperating with any government authorities. Nevertheless, cops and investigators use manipulative and coercive tactics which make them all too successful in getting people to talk to them, even when these people only provide what they assume to be innocuous information or things the government already knows.

At times, radical clients only find out about this cooperation when they receive their discovery. You may find that part of your role entails helping your client understand the potential legal ramifications of this cooperation. They may likewise be able to educate you on the political ramifications of this cooperation, as it may affect the goals they have set for their case and the legal and political strategies they want to use. If one or more of your client's codefendants cooperates after being charged, see Section 6.2 in this chapter.

2.3 Grand Juries

Grand juries are another part of the repression of radicals. Their stated purpose is to ensure indictments are filed in accordance with the law as a check against prosecutorial misconduct and abuse. In reality, they are frequently used as a fishing expedition into radical communities, networks, and movements because of their sweeping ability to ask witnesses any questions they desire in secret proceedings; this is particularly true of federal grand juries. Radicals resist grand juries to oppose the coercive, repressive nature of this process. The grand jury system is an intricate area of the law that is outside the scope of this book. There is a practice manual entitled *Representation of Witnesses Before Federal Grand Juries* that could be useful, and many lawyers who have represented grand jury resisters stress the importance of working with lawyers experienced in this area of the law.[5] Many lawyers experienced in representing grand jury resisters are active in the NLG.

The federal system and some states use grand juries as part of the process for issuing felony indictments; only the United States and Liberia still use a grand jury system, even though they originated in English common law.[6] A grand jury's involvement in your client's case might be twofold—they can operate not only as the charging body, but also as a way to attack the broader movement of which your client may be a part by gaining intelligence regarding group and individual associations. Prosecutors also use grand juries to divert movement resources into prisoner support when people are held for weeks or months on civil or criminal contempt after refusing to testify. The financial and emotional drain this creates helps the government thwart radical organizing even if they are unsuccessful in acquiring useful intelligence or confessions.

It is not unusual for movement attorneys to represent clients who have been subpoenaed to a grand jury prior

Grand Jury Resistance
by Moira Meltzer-Cohen, Esq.

As an officer of the court, you may feel uncomfortable advising your client not to cooperate with a subpoena, which represents compulsory process. The truth is that there are legal grounds for noncooperation, based on which a judge may excuse your client's testimony. It is worth standing up against a subpoena that is issued in bad faith, is a mechanism of political harassment, or attempts to intrude into the protected territory of associations, speech, or beliefs. If you have a client who wishes to resist a grand jury, rest assured that you have no legal or professional obligation to advise them to cooperate.

Particularly if you fear a perjury trap or think your client has a Fifth Amendment interest at stake, you may be obligated to advise them to remain silent before a grand jury to reduce their exposure to criminal liability!

Finally, the practice of coercive confinement—jailing grand jury resisters until they agree to cooperate with the grand jury—is likely a violation of the UN Convention Against Torture. Evidence obtained via coercive detention is inadmissible in the courts of most nations.

to indictment, who have been charged through grand juries, who have comrades who were subpoenaed before any charges were filed, or who have comrades who were being held on civil contempt when their clients were arrested. Prosecutors can also subpoena radical attorneys to grand juries, although this has been rare in the United States. Of course, the dangers of grand juries are not limited to just radicals. For example, grand juries investigating alleged gang or drug activity could be a thinly veiled attempt to gather information on communities of color, just as those investigating alleged terrorism could be attempts to gather information on Muslim communities.

If you are representing a radical client who resisted a grand jury prior to being charged, their individual experience with the grand jury may already be complete and only the criminal charges may remain. If you are representing a client who has comrades who have been subpoenaed to a grand jury and resisted, there may be a multitude of legal issues at play in the case. Collaborating with lawyers who have represented grand jury resisters is especially important in these situations. However grand juries have played a role in the case, a common experience for radicals facing charges is that they face additional stress, trauma, and feelings of isolation and paranoia due to the coercive nature of the proceedings. As their lawyer, you can play an important role in helping them navigate these situations, even if this is simply educating them about the legal landscape they are in and how to navigate their legal, personal, and political goals within it.

2.4 Private Security and Intelligence

Like police infiltrators, private intelligence firms have been used by the government and corporations to gather information and levy charges against radicals, especially those involved in environmental, Indigenous sovereignty, immigration, and labor struggles. Although these are non-governmental entities, their functioning is like governmental agencies and the role they play is part of neoliberal privatization of governmental functions. There may be a lot of evidence relevant to your defense that will require creative and persistent legal maneuvering to uncover when these entities are involved.

Some recent examples illustrate the increasing prevalence of these entities in political repression. At Standing Rock and in response to resistance to Enbridge's Line 3 pipeline, private security firms TigerSwan, Raven Executive and Security Services, and Securitas acted in collusion with law enforcement to help bring criminal charges against protesters. Similarly, Welund North America markets itself to the oil and gas industry by promising to gather surveillance on radicals to help oil and gas operators mitigate the impact of political organizing. Additionally, during widespread demonstrations against the Trump administration's family separation policy for immigrants in detention, LookingGlass Cyber Solutions was contracted by the Department of Homeland Security (DHS) to keep tabs on more than 600 planned protests.

2.5 Fascist and White Supremacist Organizations

Numerous far right militia and hate groups have emerged and/or gained power in the past several years, reinventing themselves and increasing their membership through social media, Internet chat rooms, public presentations, and confrontational rallies. Members of these groups regularly provide law enforcement with information on people they have identified as antifascists, particularly to persuade the government to press charges after confrontational protests or alleged instances of harassment of the far-right groups. This collusion is one way that these groups aid in state repression, even though they are not governmental agencies. If any of these groups have played a role in your client's case, there may be additional avenues for demanding discovery from private actors who may have provided the police, FBI, or prosecutors with exculpatory evidence.

One example of these groups is the neofascist street-fighting group Rise Above Movement (RAM), whose members publicly claimed responsibility for violence at the 2017 Unite the Right rally in Charlottesville, Virginia. RAM's members were also charged with a series of violent attacks during events in Huntington Beach, Berkeley, and San Bernardino, California, in 2017. Organizations such as this and outspoken individuals in these movements represent a growing faction of "Western chauvinists" whose campaigns of terror appeal to a hypermasculine neofascism aimed largely at alienated white men and others who align themselves with white supremacy. Although several of the most visible and violent members of these groups have faced criminal charges, these groups have historically not experienced the same level of repression that is commonly directed against antifascists or targeted racial and cultural minorities such as Muslims and immigrants.

Another example is ultra-conservative or neo-fascist independent media groups such as Project Veritas. These groups routinely collude with the government to repress antifascists, anarchists, and other radical individuals and groups. Project Veritas is funded by donors including the Trump Foundation and is one of many far-right media organizations whose members may have infiltrated your client's political circles. Groups such as this have infiltrated organizing meetings and spaces, and frequently doxx people at protests or other public gatherings.[7]

3.0 Considerations at the Outset of Cases

This section covers some common considerations at the outset of political cases. Although these are by no means unique to political prosecutions, they often play a part in cases against radicals.

3.1 Noncooperation

Not talking to cops and prosecutors is always sound legal advice for any client, yet the maxim of noncooperation may extend far beyond Miranda rights for radicals. The movements that your client comes from likely maintain a strict principle of noncooperation.[8] Many radicals consider this principle to mean more than simply not snitching; rather, it includes not assisting the government with legal action against anyone else, even those who may have harmed them. When radicals plead guilty, their attorneys can expect them to only accept noncooperating plea agreements—that is, ones that don't require the client to provide any information, either directly or indirectly, about anyone else. Often, the agreements are simply noncooperating in the way they are executed; the language of the agreement and the transcripts from the plea hearing will substantiate that the client did not share any information about others. Yet, it may be possible to construct the plea agreement to explicitly state that the client did not cooperate and will not be asked to in the future.

Nevertheless, radical clients, like all clients, benefit from instruction on their Miranda rights. If your client is in custody, it will be especially important to have a clear discussion with them as soon as possible about the necessity of not talking to anyone without first seeking your counsel. Police and prosecutors routinely use a range of tactics to try to trick arrestees into talking, such as the classic maneuvers of telling them that their codefendants are talking or claiming that they already have everything on tape. Attorneys representing radicals can help them navigate these situations by helping them prepare for this sort of subterfuge and reminding them that law enforcement can legally lie in many situations, or get away with lying if they're not explicitly permitted to do so. Many legal organizations provide "Know Your Rights" trainings and materials as a continual resource or in advance of protests to help radicals protect their rights.

3.2 Preserving Attorney-Client Privilege

All clients benefit from instruction on maintaining attorney-client privilege, although considerations for radical clients may be unique. They should fully understand all the protections of attorney-client communications as well as how there is no expectation of confidentiality with public statements, written or spoken. Your radical client may wish to make public statements or talk with their defense committee about the facts of the case. Attorneys representing radicals often have the important role to play of educating their clients on maintaining privilege so they can make good legal decisions in addition to the political decisions they may be more accustomed to. It is possible to speak publicly about the issues surrounding political repression without disclosing protected information about the facts of the case. Your client's decisions on this matter should be informed by your advice as well as by their personal, political, and legal goals.

Radical clients should also fully understand the danger of jailhouse informants; talking to anyone else in custody about the facts or situation of their case can be just as damaging as talking to the police. Similarly, they should know that prison phone lines, email, and handwritten correspondence are always monitored. It might be hard for your client to resist sharing details with someone who seems to be offering a sympathetic ear in a cold cell, or with a trusted comrade over the phone, but your encouragement of them not talking about the facts of their case outside of your conversations can help them protect their own case and look out for their comrades and political movements.

One way some movement attorneys approach these conversations is through a risk-management perspective. This perspective can help radicals make smart choices about balancing their legal, personal, and political goals, such as figuring out how to talk about the political ramifications of their charges without talking about their discovery. Radical clients must fully understand the potential negative repercussions of discussing their cases with others, both privately and publicly. Likewise, attorneys representing these defendants must understand the political benefits of taking well-considered risks to talk about their cases publicly (see chapters 4 and 5).

3.3 Bail

Radical clients may face obstacles to getting bail (or affordable bail) that might be unusual in the jurisdiction or hard for the arrestees and their communities to grapple with. At times, these obstacles are permissible under the court's rules but not necessarily employed on a regular basis; other times, the courts are simply following the standard rules to ensure high bails or no bail. Some movement attorneys have made successful bail arguments that have explicitly named these inequities.

Your client's politics and/or lifestyle may also be used

against them in ways that aren't always easy to predict. For example, some prosecutors have argued that a person facing charges is a flight risk due to their alleged membership in radical organizations or by implying that they are part of a radical network that will help them disappear. A similar argument has been that publicly advertised fundraisers for defendant support show that they have financial resources that make them more of a flight risk. Some movement attorneys have argued that these community connections and the clients' desires to vindicate themselves and their movements make them more likely to show up at their hearings. People involved in radical movements may also be transient, which might make it easier for the prosecution to claim that they are a flight risk or have no community ties.

Attorneys representing radicals and the clients themselves should be prepared for the bail hearing to turn into a full-scale attack on the client's political history and lifestyle, as well as on their movements. Many movement attorneys have taken aggressive First Amendment approaches to bail arguments when faced with attacks such as these.

3.4 Media

Political cases often gain a lot of media attention. Your client or their supporters also may have been the subject of media attention before you took the case. Regardless of whether media participation is pursued after thorough discussions between the client, the lawyer, and the client's defense committee (if applicable), or before any conversations take place, radical clients and their attorneys will benefit from clear, open communication about how media can help or hurt the client's pursuit of their legal, personal, and political goals (see chapter 5).

3.5 Political Support

Attorneys who are new to representing radicals may be surprised at the involvement of a defense committee (see chapter 4). Or they may be familiar with community defense models, such as **participatory defense**, and thus see them as a common part of working with clients. "Defense committee" is the shorthand term we often use to describe a group of supporters, community members, and/or family members of the client(s) that works in solidarity with the client(s) at various stages of their case. These efforts can include fundraising for legal and other costs, mounting political pressure and media campaigns, producing support materials such as fundraiser t-shirts and political propaganda, and providing defendants with emotional support. Although defense committees can take many forms and range from being highly active and involved to only active at certain stages, your client having one will more than likely benefit both you and your client.

4.0 Charges and Sentencing Enhancements

This section covers some common charges and sentencing

enhancements that radical clients often face, although most are by no means only used against radicals. There has also been an increasing number of state and federal laws explicitly directed at radical movements, which we explore throughout this section.

4.1 Rioting, Arson, and Looting

Rioting, arson, and looting charges are commonly levied at demonstrators during times of social unrest. The nationwide uprising that followed the death of Dr. Martin Luther King, Jr. is one historical example of such charges being used to heavily repress demonstrators. There are also numerous recent examples following the police shootings of African Americans (e.g., in Ferguson following the murder of Michael Brown, in Baltimore following the murder of Freddie Gray, in Oakland following the murder of Oscar Grant, in Minneapolis following the murder of George Floyd, in Louisville following the murder of Breonna Taylor). Arson and looting charges were widely used to repress the Ferguson uprising in 2014, and many people were harshly sentenced as a result. Rioting charges have also been used against anarchists, anticapitalists, and antifascists. It must be stressed that these charges are much more likely to be filed against people of color, and the punishments that they often receive can be significantly harsher than what their white counterparts may receive.

The Stonewall rebellion, Compton's Cafeteria Riots, and the White Night Riots were spontaneous revolts that occurred in response to LGBTQ repression. During and following such events, numerous people were brutalized by police, arrested, and faced criminal charges such as assaulting a police officer, harassment, and interfering with arrest. Importantly, these events were criminalized as riots by police and in media narratives that followed, whether or not rioting charges were actually levied.[9]

Some sociological scholars have noted a recent shift in policing and prosecutorial trends towards what one scholar terms "felonization and riotization" of protests.[10] Many states attempted to pass heavy-handed "antirioting" bills following Trump's 2017 inauguration to expand existing rioting statutes and the legal definition of "riot." In many instances, the new bills sought to create civil penalties as well. For example, in March 2019, South Dakota passed a law that creates civil penalties for what it calls "riot boosting," which is a vague phrase intended to punish anyone who "encourages" or "solicits" another's participation in a riot. Although the law appears to have been intended to target antipipeline protests, it could have incredibly far-reaching, draconian applications, particularly considering social media usage regarding political activity in the streets.

4.2 Conspiracy Charges

Radicals are not the only ones who the government targets with conspiracy charges. They are often used as a tool in drug cases, in gang cases, and against Muslim communities. Conspiracy charges have increasingly been used against radicals over the previous several decades, perhaps in part because their broad reach and loose definition make it easy to force plea agreements or secure convictions.

> **Conspiracy Statutes and Muslim Communities**
> Adapted from "Islamophobia & U.S. Surveillance Policy: A Brief Summary"
> **by Project South**
>
> Muslim communities have been aggressively targeted by conspiracy laws as part of a "preventative policing" strategy implemented by US intelligence agencies since 9/11. As Project South notes: "According to the so-called 'Radicalization Thesis' held by both national and local policing organizations, warning signs of future involvement in terrorism ('radicalization') among Muslims include: attending mosque more often, becoming more devout, growing a beard, wearing traditional attire, signs of depression or anxiety, and criticizing the policies of the U.S. government and its political allies. The entirety of the Muslim community thereby falls under suspicion without engaging in illegal or violent activity."
>
> Project South further asserts: "The federal government interprets 'the global jihadist movement' as well as various foreign organizations to be criminal conspiracies in themselves, so small acts perceived as 'in furtherance' of these 'conspiracies' can be used to cast a wide net. The 'material support' statute separately makes providing support ... to a number of crimes, including conspiracy, a federal crime. As a result of these statutes, apparently law-abiding activity—such as donating or organizing charity, translating documents, travel overseas, and providing advice or other services—can become grounds for the federal government to charge a terrorism-related offense."

Conspiracy charges are often referred to as "thought crimes" or "guilt by association" because defendants can be found guilty even without taking any action, and even if the evidence shows that they didn't have full knowledge of the alleged conspiracy. They criminalize association, speech, and politics in ways that might normally be disallowed in a courtroom. For example, someone charged with conspiracy to riot at a protest might face "evidence" of their anarchist political associations and reading material. As such, conspiracy charges often go after protest activity that is typically protected by the First Amendment, such as facilitating a meeting, distributing printed information, or creating a website.

Although the laws vary between jurisdictions, in essence, the only things the government has to prove are: 1) that some agreement to do something illegal was created; 2) at least one concrete step was taken to execute that agreement (e.g., materials purchased at a store or a web search for how to make an incendiary device); and 3) some people were in some way (even indirectly) linked to each other and the alleged conspiracy. Because so much of political organizing is a collective effort, a plain-language reading of many conspiracy statutes can cause radical clients and supporters to fear the worst possible outcome of these charges.

The fact that these charges often carry stiff penalties can assist prosecutors in forcing plea agreements. This is further complicated by the fact that it may be impossible for one defendant in a conspiracy case to sever their case through a guilty plea without implicating their codefendants because an admission of guilt validates the allegation that a conspiracy existed; alternately, the guilty plea could be to an action that the alleged conspiracy involved, even if not to the conspiracy itself. The legal mechanisms of severing a case or of one defendant pleading guilty while others plead not guilty are often quite complicated; likewise, the political and personal ramifications of these decisions and actions can be quite convoluted and devastating for radical clients. If you are representing a client who wants to plead guilty in a conspiracy case, they will likely insist on ensuring that they do not directly or indirectly cooperate against anyone. If you are representing a radical client who is not cooperating while their codefendant(s) are pleading guilty, it is imperative that the defense does not directly or indirectly revile or blame defendants who pleaded guilty.

That being said, noncooperating plea agreements may not be possible in conspiracy cases unless all alleged co-conspirators accept the plea agreement and agree to the statement of facts outlining how responsibility for the illegal actions falls on individuals and the group as a whole. As mentioned previously, radicals tend to consider noncooperating plea agreements to be ones that don't require them to provide the government with information about any other individuals or organizations, either directly or indirectly. Even when all people facing charges in a conspiracy case agree to a noncooperating plea, attorneys should be careful to ensure that no unindicted co-conspirators can be implicated.

4.3 Terrorism Charges and Enhancements

It has become increasingly common for radicals to be charged with terrorism or for terrorism enhancements to be added to the charges themselves or to the sentencing phase. Federal terrorism and material support for terrorism have also been used against radicals and in the so-called War on

Terror. A well-known law targeted at radicals is the Animal Enterprise Terrorism Act (AETA). The AETA, which was signed into law in 2006, is an expansion of the 1992 Animal Enterprise Protection Act (AEPA). These laws were written to specifically target animal rights protesters and label them terrorists. The language of the AETA criminalizes "damaging or interfering with the operations of an animal enterprise."[11] These terms are so broadly and loosely defined that they could potentially include acts such as vandalism, blocking roads, or even running a website.

Material support for terrorism is another charge that the federal government has been pursuing especially hard since 9/11. The Holy Land Foundation 5 case is a horrific example of the way that the government has used this federal law to target Muslims, in this case Palestinian Americans who ran a charity that benefited Muslims and others, both in the United States and abroad (including in Palestine). In 2004, the arrestees were charged with conspiracy to provide material support to a terrorist organization (namely, Hamas, which the federal government has designated a terrorist organization) and providing this material support; conspiracy to violate the International Emergency Economic Powers Act (IEEPA) and violating this act; conspiracy to commit money laundering and laundering money; and, for two of the people facing charges, conspiracy to file false tax returns and filing false returns. The first trial, in 2007, resulted in acquittals and mistrials on all the charges, without a single conviction; the second trial, a year later, resulted in convictions for all five defendants, with three sentenced to 15–20 years and the other two sentenced to sixty-five years. An attorney for one of the radical defendants has stressed that the government never provided any evidence against any of the accused to prove that they committed any of the charged offenses.[12]

Applying sentencing enhancements for terrorism in federal cases is another way the government can dramatically increase the amount of time your client might face. For a sentencing enhancement to stick, the government must show that the offense was "calculated to influence or affect the conduct of the government by intimidation or coercion, or to retaliate against government conduct."[13] Almost any kind of protest or dissent could be described or categorized in this way by a prosecutor, making this a particularly useful tool for the government.

A terrorism enhancement not only affects the amount of time a prisoner serves, it will most likely also affect where and how they serve it. If your client has a terrorism enhancement, it might affect their placement within the Bureau of Prisons (BOP). For example, some radicals and many Muslims who have been labeled terrorists end up in high-security units or prisons, such as the Communications Management Units (CMUs) at Terre Haute, Indiana, and Marion, Illinois.[14] These extremely restrictive units dramatically limit a prisoner's ability to have visitors, make phone calls, or otherwise communicate with the outside world. Once inside the CMU, it can be incredibly difficult to figure out how to get out of it. A terrorism enhancement will follow your client throughout their time within the BOP: it affects how guards and other prisoners interact with them; it means that their communications will be more heavily monitored, censored, and restricted; and it means that they will be closely watched by Special Investigative Services (SIS).

4.4 Laws Targeting Radicals

In this subsection, we briefly explore two types of laws that are often applied to target radicals. Broadly speaking, the criminalized behaviors can be categorized as documenting unethical acts and obscuring one's identity.

4.4.1 Ag-Gag Laws

A number of states have some form of what is known as "ag-gag" laws, which refers to laws that criminalize undercover investigations and whistleblowing regarding animal agriculture. In essence, they create fines and penalties specifically for people who film and report on the conditions inside factory farms, fur farms, research facilities, and other animal industries. These laws are becoming increasingly broad and some states have passed legislation criminalizing whistleblowing in a multitude of industries, including places such as nursing homes, hospitals, and schools.

For example, a group of animal rights protesters were charged in Utah in May 2018 with felony counts of rioting, racketeering, and theft after filming and exposing horrific conditions at a factory farm. While filming the factory farm, the protesters also rescued two piglets who were near death, bringing them to people who could rehabilitate and care for them. In Utah, the theft of any animal raised for commercial purposes constitutes a felony, regardless of the monetary value assigned to the animal or the animal's health.

4.4.2 Antimask Laws

Antimask laws are increasingly being used against radicals. People may be charged under these laws if they were alleged to have covered their faces during the time they were alleged to have committed a crime, whether this was to protect themselves and others from identification by far-right media organizations, as part of their spiritual and/or cultural practices, or for any other known or unknown reason.

Antimask laws tend to be nebulously defined. Many antimask laws were passed in the nineteenth century during tenant rights struggles and in response to violence by the Ku Klux Klan (KKK); in practice, these laws have protected the KKK and other hate groups more than those they have terrorized or murdered. The generality of these laws makes it possible for them to be applied broadly and to stifle political actions in the streets. In the late 2000s, for example, these laws were used to target people wearing Guy Fawkes masks in the Anonymous and Occupy Wall Street movements.

In recent years, antimask laws have been used against antifascist and anticapitalist struggles. These laws are one facet of newer legislation that increases the legal risk for resisting fascism in the streets. Although these legislative trends began before Trump's presidency, an increasing number of states are introducing such legislation. Despite being purportedly designed to reduce harm done in the

name of white supremacy, antimask laws most severely target those who resist racism and fascism. Many of these laws
are currently being (or have been successfully) challenged
in the courts on constitutional grounds, specifically for
violating the First and Fourteenth Amendments. This has
not always been a viable argument for political resistance in
which interpersonal violence or damage to property occurs.
Nevertheless, if your client is charged under one of these
laws, it might be a good opportunity to bring a constitutional challenge to the law.

4.5 Laws Targeting Pipeline Resistance

Starting in 2016, after protests stalled construction
of segments of the DAPL, nine states adopted laws that
increase penalties for certain crimes, making it a felony
to trespass on or disrupt "critical infrastructure," such as
pipelines and oil refineries. Several states have also drafted
bills to increase fines and jail sentences for people obstruct-
ing highways in protest of infrastructure development. At
the height of the Standing Rock protests against DAPL,
a North Dakota bill was introduced to legalize drivers
running over protesters standing in a roadway, clearing
drivers of any liability as long as their action was "unin-
tentional." North Carolina, Tennessee, Rhode Island, and
Florida introduced similar bills and, although these laws
did not pass, they illustrate chilling attempts to crush environmental and Indigenous movements.

In 2017, Oklahoma passed legislation that increased
criminal and civil penalties for trespassing on or damaging

infrastructure, as well as allowed for harsh fines for "any organization . . . found to be a conspirator with persons who are found to have committed any of the crimes."[15] The American Legislative Exchange Council (ALEC), a coalition of conservative politicians and industry representatives, developed template legislation based on Oklahoma's bill. Energy industry organizations have pushed this legislation, and many states (including Louisiana and Texas) have followed suit. Civil liberties, environmental, and Indigenous sovereignty organizations have opposed these laws as unconstitutional; at the time of this writing, lawsuits are pending in multiple states.

In 2019, the Department of Transportation issued legislation to renew the federal Pipeline Safety Act (i.e., the Pipes Act) and to continue funding the federal agency charged with implementing it, the Pipeline and Hazardous Materials Safety Administration. The Pipes Act added pipeline construction sites to the list of facilities covered by the law and increased the criminal charges against anyone "vandalizing, tampering with, impeding the operation of, disrupting the operation of, or inhibiting the operation of" an interstate oil or gas pipeline.[16]

On June 3, 2019, the Trump administration announced that it would seek to amend current legislation that prescribes a maximum penalty of twenty years in prison for damaging or destroying existing pipelines. The amendment would apply that same penalty to pipelines under construction and to disruption of pipelines.

Another way that infrastructure resistance has been targeted is with strategic lawsuits against public participation (i.e., SLAPP suits). SLAPP suits ordinarily arise from defamation lawsuits in which one person sues another for damage to reputation. Unlike typical defamation lawsuits, the SLAPP plaintiff does not necessarily plan to win their lawsuit. Rather, SLAPP suits are often intended to slow down political organizing by using the civil legal process as punishment. The deployment of SLAPP suits against environmental and animal liberation activists in the previous two decades in particular has been meant to intimidate, censor, and financially and emotionally drain protesters and their communities.

Recently, SLAPP suits have been filed against pipeline protesters in a coercive backlash against individuals and organizations who oppose Energy Transfer Partners and their destruction of the environment. In February 2019, a North Dakota judge threw out Energy Transfer Partners' suit against Greenpeace, saying it did not meet the criteria for the Racketeer Influence and Corrupt Organizations (RICO) law. The Public Participation Project is one group currently working to pass further anti-SLAPP legislation, and they offer resources for defending against SLAPP suits.[17]

4.6 Laws Targeting Immigrants and Their Advocates

Immigrants and those who stand in solidarity with them have long been targeted for their political activities. Recent years have shown an increase in anti-immigrant fervor, and the myriad implications of "zero tolerance" and family detention policies are beyond the scope of this book.

Likewise, the intricacies of immigration law and the implications of changing laws and policies on immigrants with and without documentation, those seeking asylum, and refugees is beyond the scope of this book. Any client who is not a US citizen should work with an immigration attorney in addition to their criminal defense attorney.

Resistance to the Trump administration's anti-immigration policies has been a flashpoint for many radicals in the United States. The #abolishICE movement has seen thousands of people in many cities blocking ICE detention facilities, organizing marches, and engaging in a variety of tactics to oppose increasing ICE raids and harsh detention policies, including the imprisonment of children in squalid conditions separated from their families.

State repression of the struggles in solidarity with immigrants has been grave. For example, a series of documents leaked to the media in May 2019 showed that Customs and Border Protection (CBP) was collaborating with Mexican law enforcement to increase surveillance and harassment of journalists, radicals, and attorneys in San Diego and Tijuana who were working with the Central American migrant caravan. Additionally, on July 13, 2019, Willem Van Spronsen was shot to death by police while apparently trying to set fire to deportation buses outside the Northwest Detention Center in Tacoma, Washington, a private immigration detention facility.

The longstanding faith-based humanitarian organization No More Deaths (*No Más Muertes*) has also been increasingly targeted for their efforts to aid migrants crossing through the Sonoran Desert. In May 2019, longtime

No More Deaths organizer Scott Warren went to trial after being charged with two counts of felony harboring and one count of conspiracy for allowing two undocumented men access to food, water, and a place to sleep for two nights in 2018. Warren was also one of nine arrestees to be charged in 2017 with federal misdemeanor littering charges for allegedly leaving food, water, and humanitarian aid supplies in one of the deadliest parts of the desert. In early 2019, prosecutors had secured four convictions in similar misdemeanor littering cases; the sentences were relatively light, only $250 fines plus probation, and the convictions were later overturned.

With the felony charges, Warren faced up to twenty years in prison; his trial ended in a mistrial in June 2019. He was retried in November 2019 and acquitted of all charges. A conviction was feared to be a way for the government to expand the legal definitions of "transportation" and "harboring." A conviction would have also increased the criminalization of providing future humanitarian aid, as well as increasingly criminalized anyone knowingly providing people without documents the basic necessities of life, including individuals in families with mixed immigration status who provide care for family members without documentation.

5.0 Defenses

This section briefly explores some defenses that have been used in political trials. Which defenses are available in which jurisdictions, or allowed by which judges, varies greatly; the same is true for the details of how these defenses operate in each jurisdiction. First Amendment defenses are, of course, important defenses in many political cases, as speech, ideas, and associations are often at the core of the allegations against radicals. The following defenses are often used in conjunction with First Amendment defenses.

5.1 Necessity

Necessity may be used as a defense when a client carries out an action in an effort to prevent a greater harm from occurring (e.g., ecological destruction by climate change). The necessity defense was widely used by the Catholic Worker's antinuclear Plowshares Movement, which gained notoriety in the 1980s for carrying out acts of vandalism at international nuclear facilities. Similarly, movement attorney Leonard Weinglass employed the necessity defense when representing a group of student protesters prosecuted for organizing resistance to a campus Central Intelligence Agency (CIA) recruitment drive at the University of Massachusetts in 1987. Weinglass sought to use the courtroom as an opportunity to "put the CIA on trial." He called upon government officials and former CIA operatives to testify about the CIA's role in suppressing popular movements and harming civilians. Weinglass called the CIA "a criminal enterprise" and asserted that the student activists had to break laws to oppose the CIA's worldwide atrocities. The protesters were acquitted by a jury of mostly working-class conservatives.[18]

Even though the necessity defense has historically had a low rate of acquittals, it can often be appealing to radical clients who want to center their politics within the court proceedings. At the time of this writing, however, the legal utility of necessity defense might be changing in favor of radicals to a certain extent, as there have been some recent wins (or partial wins) in climate defense cases across the country.[19]

Convincing the court to allow a necessity defense can be difficult. In certain jurisdictions, some variation of the following criteria must be met: 1) the harm caused by the defendant's actions was less than the harm that would have been caused if they had not acted; 2) the harm the defendant was trying to prevent was imminent; 3) there exists a reasonably drawn causal relationship between the defendant's actions and the harm they were trying to avoid; and 4) there was no legal alternative.[20]

Examples of recent applications of the necessity defense include the 2015 Flood Wall Street 11 case, the 2016 Delta Five case, the 2015 case of Chiara D'Angelo, and the 2016 Valve Turner case. In September 2019, the Washington Supreme Court denied the government's petition for review of an appellate court decision reversing and remanding a case in which the trial court denied a defendant's request to use the necessity defense at trial. This was an encouraging legal development for future cases in Washington State. Much remains to be seen about how this legal landscape will change in the future, but there have been positive gains in recent years.

The necessity defense has been popular in some movements, less for its legal strength and more for its moral and political strength. For some radical environmentalists, for example, winning their legal cases is not always a priority, even when getting convicted entails prison time. This can be a challenging situation for some lawyers to understand, but often lawyers representing radical clients must figure out how to help their clients achieve their overall goals even when this means pursuing less-than-optimal defenses or otherwise risking an adverse outcome at trial.

5.2 Entrapment

Local police and the FBI routinely target and entrap radicals, charging them with high-profile crimes. These tactics have been well honed in the so-called War on Terror.[21] The charges often include conspiracy and terrorism, and attorneys representing radicals are likely to be confronted with these cases.

The story is by now all-too familiar. An informant is sent into a community, befriends people, creates a conspiracy, and ropes other people into it. These informants often take advantage of people who are the most disadvantaged—young people, people fighting addiction, or people struggling with poverty, homelessness, and/or mental illness. The informants can foster dependency in them, such as by supplying them with drugs or alcohol, a place to live, or a job. And they almost always provide the means by which the conspiracy can be accomplished (e.g., the bomb, transportation, funding, et cetera). Although this might constitute entrapment in the public mind, in most jurisdictions, none of this constitutes entrapment in the legal sense.

If your client has been entrapped, you will both most likely face an uphill battle. Notably, the entrapment defense has not been used successfully at trial in a federal terrorism case since 9/11.[22] In some cases, some jurors have stated postconviction that they saw evidence of entrapment but were still unable to acquit based on the jury instructions. Despite the inherent difficulties in presenting this affirmative defense, some radical clients may find that incorporating an entrapment argument can be worthwhile—both in the courtroom and in the public sphere. For example, entrapment can show that the case is not just about your client but is about their wider movement and about political repression. As people are often entrapped after being targeted for their politics or involvement in political struggles, making these arguments to a jury or in the public sphere can often be relatively easy. For example, it can be easy to demonstrate how the person facing charges became a person of interest in an investigation after something they said or wrote was noticed by the government, or after the government had sent an informant into their community or movement.

If you and your client decide to engage the media, the entrapment defense may feel like fighting the same battle on two vastly different fronts. In the public mind, entrapment often simply means that the government created a crime and pushed someone into it. In legal terms, however, entrapment can be nearly impossible to prove. In some ways, this can make success on the public front easier than the legal battle. If a media campaign is used alongside an entrapment defense, coordination between the two would likely be beneficial. Chapter 5 offers more insights into how media campaigns can work alongside legal approaches to cases.

5.3 Mutual Combat

Mutual combat could be easily confused with self-defense, but they are distinct. Case law in California provides clarifying language in that jurisdiction: mutual combat means "not merely a reciprocal exchange of blows but one pursuant to mutual intention, consent, or agreement preceding the initiation of hostilities. . . . In other words, it is not merely the combat, but the preexisting intention to engage in it, that must be mutual."[23] Self-defense, in contrast, refers to a response to an attack that was initiated without an agreement to participate in combat.

Mutual combat is an unusual area of the law that might have some appeal to radical people facing charges from physical confrontations, which has been an element of antifascist counterprotests of white supremacists. The term "mutual combat" is not used in every jurisdiction and its meaning can vary, so other terms that point to the same or similar defenses might be applicable in your jurisdiction.

A recent example from California can help illustrate the potential of this defense and suggest how it might continue to be an option for radical clients. On June 26, 2016, at least 10 people were hospitalized in Sacramento after antifascists confronted a publicly announced neo-Nazi rally at the state capitol. Many of the hospitalizations were the result of stab wounds inflicted by neo-Nazis on antifascists. Almost a year after the confrontation, local police arrested three antifascist protesters and one neo-Nazi on a variety of charges, including assault with a deadly weapon or by means of force likely to inflict great bodily injury. Attorneys for the antifascists announced soon after the charges were filed that they would be pursuing a defense based on mutual combat, although the defense went untested when the defendants took a noncooperating plea deal in November 2019. Given the alarming rise of the alt-right and neo-Nazi/fascist activity since the election of Trump, it is likely that these kinds of confrontations will increase and escalate.

Although mutual combat is potentially a viable defense, it does not have an agreed-upon definition in some jurisdictions; there also does not appear to be concrete case law about its applicability across the board. In some jurisdictions, the conduct that could be described by the term "mutual combat" might itself be an offense.

6.0 Joint Defenses

Radical movements are relational, and thus cases against radicals often involve codefendants. There are benefits to mounting a joint defense for both you and your client, including financial, emotional, and resource benefits. It is important to note that joint defense doesn't always mean that each individual client takes the same legal approach to their cases; rather, it means that there are shared agreements about how best to meet the legal and political goals of each individual client and their codefendants.

Some lawyers may believe that a joint defense will conflict with ethical standards that effectively serve the needs of their clients. At its best, ethical training can enable lawyers to protect each of their individual clients and prevent conflicts of interest among clients. Radical clients may have larger social and political goals when fighting their charges that are best served by this form of collaboration, so joint defenses can be a way of providing representation that is in their best interests. Keeping this movement perspective and clients' overall goals in mind may help lawyers sort through the ethical obligations when mounting a joint defense.

Many movement attorneys have found joint defense agreements both useful and necessary when working with other counsel.[24] Joint defense agreements can be helpful in navigating the complexities that could arise from this sort of collaboration. These are important even if some of the people facing charges pursue different legal strategies.

At times, lawyers may represent more than one defendant in a case, although this is much more common with low-level protest charges than more serious offenses. Nevertheless, many movement attorneys and radical clients have found it worthwhile to manage the conflicts of interest that arise with dual representation. The NLG is a useful resource for coordinating with lawyers experienced in the variety of approaches to joint defense and dual representation.

6.1 Balancing the Needs of Your Client's Codefendants

The topic of this subsection may seem to conflict with your ethical obligations to provide your clients with the best possible defense. To provide your client with the best defense while considering the needs of their codefendants requires a shift in framework. When representing radicals, "best possible defense" can mean situating your client's case in a larger political struggle. From this perspective, your duty of loyalty to your client can be considered as broader than their individual case and legal goals; applying your ethical obligations to the entirety of your client's goals and interests can allow for stronger representation.

Provided a client's goals are not directly harmful to other individuals, lawyers can consider supporting their individual client's legal, personal, and political goals to be in their client's best interests. This remains true even when the implications of approaching representation in this way may seem to conflict with traditional ethical training. Likewise, this remains true when your client's goals include considering and supporting their codefendants' needs, goals, and priorities. Although taking this approach might seem to be controversial or counter to traditional representation, it can squarely be a part of ethical representation and important to providing the best defense.[25]

Once clients have decided that they want a joint case, they may want their attorneys to work with everyone's interests in mind, in balance with the standard ethical obligations to the individuals. This approach can often be balanced successfully by considering the needs and interests of all defendants from a collective perspective. That is, attorneys can consider the ways in which they can craft legal strategies for their clients that help all the defendants fight back against the prosecution's efforts at repressing political movements and punishing individuals involved in those movements.

Yet, there are several ways that clients and their attorneys might inadvertently damage codefendants' cases. On a basic level, attorneys representing radical defendants must remember to be careful in motions, briefs, at hearings, and in the media with how they talk about codefendants and others. They should take care to never implicate others, disparage them, or imply that their clients are not like the "real criminals" or "bad/violent protesters."

Being careful with these basic considerations can become incredibly difficult as cases progress, especially when one or a few people facing charges may face much less damaging evidence than others. Even when in a better legal position, many radical clients will not want their charges dropped, their case severed, or their case resolved through an individual plea agreement if that beneficial development for them will make things worse for others. They may consider their overall interests to be served much better by remaining in the pool as long as possible; for example, their participation in a joint trial might create opportunities to discredit the evidence against the other radicals, or at least to make the prosecutor worried that the evidence might be discredited in the jurors' minds.

There are numerous benefits to a collective defense. Certainly, there is strength in numbers. Often, when cases are split up, defendants are more vulnerable to convictions and harsh punishment. Sticking together may also give the group more bargaining power, as well as help group members who are more vulnerable to conviction avoid more severe consequences. Many movement attorneys also find value in taking collective approaches to defense; fighting charges as a group can allow for strategic wins in the courtroom that aid political movements in the streets. Even so, there may be legitimate reasons that people facing charges need or want their case to be handled separately, as well as many ways to do this that are not at others' expense.

6.2 Cooperating Defendants

As is true of many people facing charges, your client may be under intense pressure to snitch on their codefendants in exchange for a lighter sentence. It is important to remember that radical movements do not condone or encourage snitching; for attorneys, this means that radicals expect them not to pressure clients to cooperate against others, even if doing so might benefit them legally.

Nevertheless, if your client decides to cooperate, it is important to understand how to minimize the harm to the remaining codefendants and their movements. Some things to pay special attention to include statements made in proffers, statements of fact in a plea agreement, and statements made to the press. Attorneys for cooperating clients can be well positioned to take steps to limit the fallout while meeting their ethical obligations to their clients. Additionally, cooperating defendants may face a withdrawal of political and financial support from others.

Ethical Obligation to the Greater Good
by Dennis Cunningham, Esq.

As lawyers, we have it drilled into us that we owe a duty of representation to each client, the rest of the world be damned. If something would make us hesitate before attacking anyone else's interests, our loyalties are said to be divided and we are supposed to avoid taking the case, or withdraw.

But wait: Our political clients want and deserve to be represented on a political basis. If a client to whom we owe such unflinching duty demands it, we owe a broader duty to the client's community or activist group to receive input from and account to their community; show solicitude for the welfare of others in it; act in ways that promote the *esprit* and effectiveness of the community; and take care not to undermine its values, or the goals of the client's activism.

Call it intersectional lawyering. No adversary has ever tried to pierce the attorney-client privilege because I met in solidarity with fellow plaintiffs, defendants, or legal supporters. My amazing activist clients have always been my teachers and comrades, helping me hone this praxis; and for it, we have all been the wiser, happier, and freer.

7.0 Considerations for Resolving the Charges

Radical clients tend to consider their legal, personal, and political goals when determining resolutions to their cases. Attorneys are well positioned to help their clients pursue all their goals, including through motions and other arguments that may be just as effective as trial, or more so. And, of course, radical clients and attorneys should always ensure that other people are not adversely affected by the resolution of a case.

7.1 Going to Trial

Even though the criminal legal system pressures defendants to settle their cases without going to trial, radical clients may want a trial even when they will almost certainly be convicted. Trial may play an important role in pursuing their overall goals, regardless of the legal outcome. Although their attorneys always have the duty of presenting sound legal information, advice, and perspectives on their clients' options, attorneys representing radicals can benefit from keeping all their clients' goals in mind when evaluating these options. There may be benefits of going to trial that are not apparent at first. There are also times when radical clients will choose their personal and/or political goals over legal goals or self-interest, which may be frustrating for attorneys. This can be especially frustrating when there is disagreement or misunderstanding about which goals and priorities are desirable given the circumstances.

When the client desires a trial, the challenge for the attorney may be figuring out a trial strategy that will help the client work towards all their goals in addition to figuring out how to provide the best possible defense.

7.2 Noncooperating Plea Agreements

When a radical client wants a plea agreement, their attorney should only negotiate a noncooperating plea agreement that does not inadvertently implicate codefendants or unindicted persons. As previously discussed, it is generally of utmost importance to radicals to maintain the principle of noncooperation with the government.

Noncooperating Plea Agreements: The Case of Michael "Rattler" Markus
by Sandra Freeman, Esq.

Michael "Rattler" Markus is an Oglala Lakota and former Marine who never engaged in protest before the late summer of 2016, when he went to Oceti Sakowin near the Standing Rock reservation to aid in stopping the construction of Dakota Access Pipeline (DAPL) and the desecration of Lakota treaty land and sacred sites. The federal government indicted Rattler and several other Indigenous water protectors who helped protect thousands of protesters from a militarized police raid in October 2016.

Even though he admitted to pouring gasoline on a barricade to stop the police from advancing, Rattler had many constitutional, statutory, and treaty-based defenses to the charges of civil disorder and use of fire in the commission of a federal felony (which has a ten-year mandatory minimum). The defense team remained client centered: Rattler's personal and political goals guided our approach to understanding the evidence and developing case strategies and priorities.

Working from a place of mutual learning, respect, and support enabled Rattler and the defense team to craft a noncooperating plea agreement that made his noncooperation clear while providing him with a forum to begin to tell the true story of his involvement at Standing Rock. This plea allowed the coercive use of fire charge to be dropped while making it clear that he was not disavowing the reasons he and other water protectors came to Standing Rock. Similarly, this plea allowed him to assert that he was not relinquishing the rights of Indigenous sovereignty or in any way assisting the government's continued surveillance, prosecution, and repression of Indigenous people acting in defense of the water and land.

Radical clients and lawyers should also ensure that there is a clear agreement in place. There have regrettably been some political cases in which unspecified plea agreements were entered and had severe negative consequences for the clients. An especially egregious example of the danger of such agreements is from an entrapment case arising out of the Occupy Wall Street movement. In this case, the three people facing charges who pleaded guilty did so without their lawyers specifying any of the terms of the agreement. At sentencing, they were given not only years in prison, but also a *lifetime* of supervised release. They were all in their early to mid-twenties when they were sentenced, which had significant consequences for the individual defendants, their loved ones, and the Occupy movement.

Your client would likely benefit greatly from a thorough discussion of all direct and indirect consequences of a plea agreement. Some examples include convictions that prevent them from going into specific lines of work, securing housing, or legally owning a firearm. Other examples include probation conditions that limit their political activity or associations with other radicals (particularly others with felony convictions), fines or restitution going to the institutions they were protesting against, restriction of access to computers, and open doorways for the FBI or prosecutors to question them about other open or future cases.

Radical clients may desire terms of a plea agreement that are unusual or may not seem sensible. For example, some radicals have negotiated plea agreements with executed jail/prison terms with no probation afterwards rather than agreeing to sentences of probation only, without imprisonment. Many radicals have opted for short-term incarceration over lengthy restrictions on their movements, associations, and political organizing, which has led them to choose jail over monitoring. Although these pleas are not always available, seeking them might seem counterintuitive to lawyers or may not even come to mind as a possibility. Taking a creative approach to discussing with clients all the options, even atypical ones, can be an important part of providing them with the best possible representation.

Chapter 3: Working with Radical Clients

Chapter Outline

1.0 Lawyering in Solidarity With Radical Clients

In chapter 1, we highlighted ways in which working with radical clients can differ from traditional criminal defense. In this chapter, we dig deeper into these topics and what it means to work in solidarity with radical clients—that is, together in shared struggle, each having distinct roles to play in fighting back against State repression.

If this is your first time representing a radical client, you might find yourself thinking in new and different ways about legal strategy, your attorney-client relationship and interpersonal dynamics, and what it means to "win." We hope this chapter will help prepare you for these challenges if this type of lawyering is new, or help you work even more effectively in shared struggle if you have been doing this for a while.

Representing radicals often means engaging in a political project in addition to traditional legal representation. This does not necessarily mean that you and your client will share political analyses or even discuss the politics of the case all that often. But it may mean that you and your client figure out ways of centering the politics of the case in every legal maneuver. Your client's politics may also be developing throughout the ordeal; fighting charges and confronting governmental mechanisms of repression is often a radicalizing experience.

Whatever the situation, this approach to lawyering will undoubtedly mean relating to your client on as equal footing as possible to help counter the dehumanizing and demoralizing experience of fighting charges. This perspective should be held as you continue to provide the robust defense you would provide for any client. This may entail things like helping demystify the criminal legal system for your client and their supporters, or advocating for them in the face of oppressive practices within the court (e.g., ensuring their correct gender pronouns are used, ensuring their physical and medical access needs are met, et cetera).

Thinking about your interactions with your client as similar to interactions between team members with equally important but distinct skill sets may help you see the ways that working with radical clients can be mutually beneficial. Each of you have distinct roles, areas of responsibility, and decision-making authority. Approaching the attorney-client relationship in this way may require broadening the typical understanding of the attorney-client relationship, but working as a team you can get much more accomplished. Many times, for example, radical clients have prior experience with fighting charges that stem from political actions or from campaigns of state repression. They also may know or have access to a large network of radicals who have fought similar charges, or may be working with them directly throughout their case (e.g., through a defense committee). Even if they are facing charges for the first time, they may have well-developed political analyses of the court system, the police, prisons, corporations, and the government. Thus, it is important not to underestimate radical clients' knowledge and experience.

Many times, radical clients hold political analyses that are critical of or hostile to governmental, legal, financial, and social power structures. You may or may not hold the same or even similar political analyses. Coming to agreement on your politics is not required to work effectively with your client or to ensure that you provide robust representation, but coming to an understanding of each other's politics and beliefs may help you navigate disagreements or areas in which your priorities are not aligned. No matter how aligned your belief systems, you will likely have important legal insights that will help your clients make legal decisions, just as their goals and priorities will likely help you create strong legal strategies for their defense. Developing this shared understanding can help you create a wider range of legal options and potential strategies than may have been apparent without this understanding.

A word about watching out for your own prejudices, preconceptions, assumptions, and socialized behaviors is necessary here as well. Recognizing the privileges we carry and the ways that can shape our interactions with others, as well as others' experiences of our actions and statements, can be incredibly difficult and is a lifelong project of

growth and learning. Paying attention to the ways we interact with others is often even harder when we're under stress
and the stakes are high. One privilege that every attorney
has is the legal and social status of being a lawyer. Although
this status is obviously a necessary part of providing criminal defense, it can be important to ensure that this status
does not equate to coercive power over your client. There is
a subtle but important difference between drawing on your
skills and expertise as a lawyer when advising your client on
legal decisions and drawing on the authority of your law
degree to tell them what is best for their personal or political goals. Navigating these differences can be incredibly
challenging and nuanced, and is often an important part of
representing radical clients. The example questions in chapter 1 will likely help you understand, clarify, and center your
radical client's goals, priorities, and needs.

1.1 Representation Agreements

Many movement attorneys we've worked with over the
years have stressed the importance of having clear, detailed
representation agreements in place as soon as the attorney-
client relationship is established. An example is provided
on our website.[1] This practice is by no means unique to
representing radical defendants, and instructions on how
to construct agreements is beyond the scope of this book.
Throughout this book, however, we recommend elements
that have been considered in representation agreements with
radicals or that have been suggested by lawyers who we've

worked with over the years. We hope they will help both you and your radical client work together more effectively.

1.2 Communicating Boundaries, Expectations, and Commitments

As with any client, being clear at the outset about what you will do, what you won't do, and what you can't do as a legal professional is important when representing radical clients. If you feel political affinity with your client, what you communicate might also be about your personal and political boundaries or commitments. Your client may also want you to help them fight back against state repression in all the ways they are used to (e.g., criminal defense, organizing campaigns, protesting in the streets, civil litigation, policy work, et cetera), which you may or may not be interested in or able to do.

Clarifying your boundaries and commitments is useful at the outset, as is re-evaluating them as the legal situation changes. They can also be reflected in your representation agreement. For example, if your practice includes both criminal defense and civil rights litigation, you might not initially be willing to commit to filing a lawsuit about unlawful arrest, but might be interested in this if the criminal charges get thrown out or your client is acquitted. As recommended previously, talking explicitly with your client about future litigation and determining which representation agreements need to be in place for various types of cases can help ensure you both stay on the same page about how long and in which ways you'll be working together.

These considerations are not being presented with the assumption that you only have this one client, of course. As with any client, keeping open lines of communication regarding deadlines for motions and responses, any extensions or schedule changes you need to request, and any delays from the prosecution or judge is important. If your client is working with a defense committee or other supporters to generate media about the case, fundraise, or organize court support, legal updates often have a significant impact on the political organizing happening around the case. Keeping your client informed can help them address their other goals and priorities for their case. Having open communication about delays and extensions can be especially important with clients who are incarcerated, as being locked up makes the entire process even more emotionally taxing.

Finally, communicating what you need and expect of your client is just as important with radical clients as it is with any other criminal defendants. Your client may continue to be active in political organizing unrelated to their pending charges, be busy working a lot, or be overwhelmed by commitments to family members, and may benefit from clear communication from you about what would make it easier to provide them with strong representation.

1.3 Facilitating Client Participation

Another important way of working with radical clients in shared struggle is ensuring they can participate in their own defenses as much as they desire. Radical clients are often highly motivated to participate actively in their case (or case resolution, if there is a plea agreement). Individuals vary, of course, and interest in or emotional capacity for being active participants in the legal proceedings can also change throughout the course of any case. Yet, many radical clients will want to be active in all aspects of their legal defense preparations and decision making.

1.3.1 Accessing Discovery

Many radical clients will want full and continuous access to their discovery. If you work in a jurisdiction that typically restricts or makes it difficult to access discovery, figuring out ways of ensuring full access will be important. Radical clients are often concerned not only about what their discovery means for them, but also about what it means for their comrades and movements. Thus, the government surveillance, alleged evidence, and informant testimony and reports may be important to your client for reasons aside from their individual legal interests, even if that information needs to stay private and/or privileged until the case is resolved. Making sure clients understand the implications and potential consequences of publicly sharing discovery while cases are pending can also be important.

1.3.2 Assisting With Preparing Motions and Arguments

Radical clients may want to be involved in crafting the language used in motions and legal arguments to be sure the language aligns with their politics, political priorities for framing their cases, and their desires to not implicate or otherwise harm others. This may include ensuring that political movements and the people involved in them are discussed in truthful and respectful ways. For example, it will be important to radical clients that anyone mentioned in motions and arguments is referred to by the correct gender pronoun and has their racial or ethnic identities talked about appropriately.

Many radical clients will also want to ensure that motions and arguments do not imply or concede political or personal associations, organizational memberships, or any individual's presence at specific events. Many of these types of considerations will be readily apparent to lawyers because they are clearly allegations that the government has the burden of proving. Yet, others may not be as readily apparent. For example, the government may refer to the group of people it's targeting as an organization and rely on that assumption in its theory of the case. Nevertheless, the person facing charges may not be willing to concede that assumption in written or oral arguments because it is not accurate (e.g., there were just friends hanging out, not meetings of an organization) and because it facilitates the government's attempt to criminalize political organizing. Radical clients may be attuned to nuances such as these because they are often all too familiar with how state repression works.

Further, radical clients are often attuned to language that may support their defense at the expense of others, whether that means codefendants, unindicted radicals, or movements in a broader sense. We explore the importance of not vilifying other radicals in the next subsection.

1.4 Crafting Legal Strategies in Support of Movements

As we mentioned in chapter 1, there are many organizations whose efforts include fighting laws that target radicals, such as the NLG and L4BL. Organizations such as these can spend decades fighting charges and strategizing ways to minimize their impacts. Connecting with these organizations can be invaluable when representing a radical client, as well as throughout one's legal career. Lawyers and legal workers in these organizations often have a great deal of experience and expertise in crafting legal strategies that not only defend clients well, but also help protect social movements.

As a lawyer representing a radical client, an important part of working in solidarity with your client is ensuring that the legal strategies you devise are not at the expense of other radicals, political organizations, or political movements. Avoiding strategies that rely on pointing at your client's codefendants or someone else identifiable in the discovery is generally easy, of course. What can be more challenging is devising legal strategies and the language for arguments that legitimize your client as a person, as someone with anti-oppressive and/or antiauthoritarian political beliefs, and as a participant in a radical social movement. Likewise, finding strategies and language that legitimize radical social movements and their goals can be challenging.

For example, you may want to talk about a client charged with locking themselves to pipeline construction equipment as foolish, childish, misguided, or rash in an

Representing Puerto Rican *Independentistas* Who Rejected the Jurisdiction of the US Courts
by Jan Susler, Esq., People's Law Office (PLO)

A federal court jury found 10 suspected members of the Puerto Rican terrorist group FALN guilty today on charges arising from bombings and attempted bombings in the Chicago area. . . . They each face possible sentences of up to 80 years in prison. . . . The defendants were not in court after the trial opened a week ago, when they disrupted proceedings and contended they could not be tried in U.S. courts because they were prisoners of war in their fight for Puerto Rican independence.[*]

You cannot expect law school to prepare you for working with revolutionary people who understand the US courts as a tool in the government's arsenal for maintaining colonial control over their nation. Your best teachers are those very revolutionaries who orient themselves within a long history of struggle and who have laid their lives on the line to oppose colonial control. The *Independentistas* viewed their arrest, prosecution, and imprisonment as opportunities to expose the colonial relationship between the United States and Puerto Rico: to challenge the notion of one nation denying another's sovereignty and self-determination. They refused to defend themselves in what they perceived as illegal proceedings.

Instead, they oriented us legal advisors—not considering us defense attorneys—to their needs: namely, to work with them to present their case in international fora; couch their position in international law such as the Geneva Convention, and expose the discriminatory and politically vindictive treatment they were subjected to as a result of their position. In other words, put US colonialism on trial. We are so privileged to have been able to work with such freedom fighters.

[*] "Ten Puerto Ricans Convicted in U.S. Bombings," *The Washington Post*, February 12, 1981, page A7.

attempt to appeal to the jury on an emotional level and create sympathy for the young person sitting at the table in front of them. But, there are other ways of talking about the relevant legal points that need to be made without casting your client, their peers, or radical political movements in a negative light. Finding these ways is an important part of representing radicals.

Similarly, it can be easy but imprudent for lawyers representing radical clients to make arguments that imply or state explicitly that there were "bad protesters" who did the things that your client has been charged with, but your client is not one of "them." It is also important to avoid referring to other participants in resistance movements as the "real criminals" who should be arrested, convicted, or imprisoned. Vilifying other radicals does not need to be a part of providing a robust criminal defense for radical clients.

This language is unfortunately common in political commentary (e.g., editorials, blogs, news commentary) and in internal disputes within leftist and antiauthoritarian circles, but it should not be used in the criminal defense of radicals. Talking about others' conduct or actions is likely not relevant to your client's defense and is thus relatively easy to avoid in a legal sense. Even if it could be useful on an emotional or intellectual level when attempting to persuade the judge or jury, it is important to remain in solidarity with your client and their movements by not vilifying others. Many radical clients will stress the importance of this consideration in any arguments being made in their defense.

2.0 Considerations for Clients at Higher Risk

Often, defendants have identities, needs, and life circumstances that can put them at greater risk while interfacing with the criminal legal system. In this section, we outline common scenarios you may encounter when working with radical defendants. Because these higher-risk situations are by no means unique to radical clients, we focus on how these situations can be of particular relevance to people facing charges due to their political ideas and actions.

When possible, we have offered starting points for additional resources for many of these situations, although space limitations do not allow for an exhaustive listing of all potential resources across the country.

2.1 Pretrial Incarceration

Pretrial incarceration is designed to be devastating to *all* prisoners, and radical clients are no exception. Often, radicals have access to support that many prisoners do not, such as visits, regular mail, and commissary funds. However, they may be targeted by guards, administrators, and other prisoners for their race, gender or other identities, political beliefs, political associations, or refusal to join gangs. For example, a trans defendant may be placed in a jail according to their **assigned gender** but not their gender identity, or they may be housed in segregation because of their gender identity. Or, a white antiracist defendant may face harassment from other prisoners for refusing to join a white supremacist gang. Attorneys representing radicals might find that their clients need additional legal support (e.g., transfer out of segregation after being punished for their political affiliations), emotional support (e.g., visits from a chosen spiritual advisor), or physical support (e.g., medical care after getting attacked, access to gender-affirming medical care, et cetera). If your client has a defense committee, another form of political support (e.g., a nonprofit serving trans prisoners nationally), or loved ones who are able to visit them in jail, they might have a variety of resources to draw on to help protect and support them while in custody. Being prepared to help clients through a myriad of problems while incarcerated pretrial can help them be able to participate fully in their legal defense.

2.1.1 Codefendants Incarcerated Separately

When codefendants are incarcerated in different units or facilities and want to use a joint defense approach to their cases, their lawyers may have to facilitate conversations between them. Attorneys may also need to find ways for the defendants to review their discovery and prepare any joint defenses together in person. The rules governing what is permissible vary greatly across jurisdictions and facilities, but figuring out how to make this (or useful alternatives) happen may be more of a priority for radical defendants than other criminal defendants.

2.1.2 Political Organizing Behind Bars

Radical defendants often initiate or take part in political organizing or actions while incarcerated, whether this is for personal needs such as access to vegan food or necessary medications, or for collective reasons such as access to visits, phone calls, and healthcare for all the prisoners at their facility. Tactics that prisoners might employ include refusing to lock down, work strikes, hunger strikes, boycotting phone or commissary systems, and so on. Many times, engaging in these tactics or even being suspected of political organizing can carry grave consequences for prisoners. Depending on the punishments that the guards mete out, prisoners resisting conditions on the inside could find access to their discovery, to visits and phone calls, or to you as their lawyer restricted or explicitly banned (officially or unofficially). Preparing for the possibility of advocating for your client in these situations is an important consideration when representing radical clients, as is advising them on possible consequences of any actions that could be deemed to be in violation of rules, policies, or laws.

Outside attention being brought to the conditions inside the jail is a common part of political organizing behind bars. Prisoners often work with supporters to create media campaigns or political pressure campaigns. These efforts can be instrumental in getting the conditions on the inside changed, and it's common for the guards to punish anyone they consider to be a leader or to be connected to radicals on the outside. As an attorney representing a radical client, you may have the opportunity and desire to support these efforts, such as by speaking to the media about the conditions your client is facing. Even if you are not interested or willing to be involved, having open communication with your client and their defense committee or other supporters can help ensure you're able to work well together and understand everything that is going on for your client.

2.1.3 Political Persecution Behind Bars

Radical clients incarcerated pretrial often find themselves routinely harassed by guards and administrators because of their values (assumed or expressed), the specific charges they are facing, or their affiliations with radical movements or other radical prisoners. This persecution could take the form of being denied work assignments or other designations, being written up constantly for alleged disciplinary infractions, being denied their mail, being moved or having their cells searched frequently, being placed in situations where they're likely to be attacked, and so on. Again, preparing for this possibility is helpful when representing radicals and may be an important part of providing them with effective representation.

2.2 People of Color

The prison-industrial complex specifically represses people of color, for whom jails and prisons can be especially dangerous. In addition to being targeted for their politics and alleged political activities, radicals of color are often subject to increased violence and persecution by prosecutors, judges, guards, or other prisoners. Sentencing and plea offers are also routinely worse for people of color than their white counterparts. Attorneys representing radicals of color should be especially aware of how their clients can be treated worse than normal at every step, particularly if these attorneys are white and haven't experienced racist oppression directly.

There are many legal and political organizations that may be able to offer support and assistance to people of color who are facing charges and/or incarcerated, as well as their attorneys. Among these organizations are Asian American Legal Defense and Education Fund, Asian Americans Advancing Justice, Black Movement-Law Project, Lakota People's Law Project, L4BL, National Conference of Black Lawyers (NCBL), Southern Poverty Law Center (SPLC), and Water Protector Legal Collective (WPLC). The United People of Color Caucus (TU-POCC) and Anti-Racism Committee (ARC) of the NLG are networks of progressive lawyers that also might offer resources or have recommendations for local or national organizations.

2.3 Immigration Status

Permanent residents, people in the country with documentation, and people without documentation can suffer additional consequences and complications after arrest. Clients in any of these situations should be immediately connected with immigration support services, including consulting with an immigration attorney. Common situations they may face include being placed on ICE holds and remaining in custody when they otherwise would have been released, being subject to immigration proceedings at the conclusion of their case, or being denied residency or citizenship due to convictions. At the time of this writing, legal situations for immigrants, refugees, and asylum seekers in the United States are rapidly worsening and the law is quickly changing, with attempts to align policies with xenophobic political agendas increasing in ferocity.

The following organizations have a variety of resources for attorneys working at the intersection of criminal defense and immigration law: *Al Otro Lado*, the Immigration Advocates Network's National Immigration Legal Services Directory, the Immigrant Defense Project, the National Immigration Law Center, the National Immigration Project (NIP) of the NLG, Project South, South Asian Americans Leading Together (SAALT), the Queer Detainee Empowerment Project, and No More Deaths.

2.4 Muslims and the War on Terror

Muslims and people from the Middle East or nearby regions have continued to be targeted, particularly by the federal government, since the start of the so-called War on Terror. Not everyone scapegoated is Muslim (many Sikhs have been targeted, harassed, attacked, persecuted, or charged while being called Muslims) or Arab, as racist xenophobia in the United States does not require understanding of cultures, ethnic identities, or religions seen as "other." Radical clients from these backgrounds or who have these identity markers might be targeted based on these prejudices as well as their other identities (e.g., people of color, people who are not citizens, et cetera).

Resources for supporting radical clients experiencing this targeting include the Center for Constitutional Rights, The Constitutional Law Center for Muslims in America, CUNY CLEAR (City University of New York's Creating Law Enforcement Accountability & Responsibility), and Project South.

2.5 Transgender People and People Outside the Gender Binary

The criminal legal system reinforces rigid and violent gender categories. Trans, gender-nonconforming, **intersex**, and queer radicals can be subject to harsher treatment in jail, prison, and the courts.[2] One of the ways this disparity is evident is in queer and trans folks being disproportionately detained, harassed, and sexually assaulted by police and being more often subject to violence and harassment while incarcerated. The brutality of this system occurs in less overt ways too, such as in legal paperwork, in which a client's correct name, pronouns, and gender identity may not be respected, and in carceral facilities, in which prisoners are typically housed based on their birth-assigned gender or in segregation, regardless of their current identity or appearance. Trans and gender-nonconforming people may use oral, topical, or injectable hormone medications, and may have difficulty accessing this care while incarcerated or be prevented from accessing it entirely. Attorneys representing these clients must understand the potential obstacles and threats their clients may face during the course of their cases, and advocate for their needs.

The Sylvia Rivera Law Project provides a wealth of information and training. Their tip sheet "Supporting Incarcerated Transgender and Gender Non-Conforming People" is an excellent starting point.[3] Other resources include GLAD Legal Advocates & Defenders, the LGBT Bar Association and Foundation, the TGI Justice Project, the Transformative Justice Law Project, and the Transgender Law Center.

2.6 People With Dependents (Legal or Otherwise)

People with dependents often have extra needs, priorities, and responsibilities to consider; the government routinely uses these as points of leverage over defendants to force plea agreements and/or coerce people into cooperating against their comrades. This is true whether the dependents are children, elders, or other adults in their lives who need their dedicated assistance. Likewise, this is true whether the relationship between a defendant and their dependent(s) has legal status (e.g., parent, legal guardian, medical power of attorney) or is not legally recognized.

For queer and trans people, there may be even more risk; for example, several states bar people with criminal records from fostering or adopting children. Because queer and trans parents may lack biological ties to their children, they are often not afforded the meager legal protections that incarcerated biological parents may have. Additionally, queer and trans people may be more likely than their straight counterparts to live with and rely on a non-nuclear family structure to meet their basic needs. Your queer or trans client may be part of a chosen family composed of other queer and trans adults whose access to housing, employment, and basic necessities of survival are tied up with those of your client, and their incarceration can pose a significant obstacle for those family members as well, regardless of whether they are legally considered to be dependents.

Attorneys representing radical clients in any of these situations should take extra care to help them find resources for meeting their needs, which often fall in disparate areas of the law (e.g., family law, et cetera). A good starting point to find resources is Legal Services for Prisoners with Children (LSPC).

2.7 Mental Health Needs

Prisoners with mental health needs can suffer intensely when incarcerated and may face severe dangers to their health, well-being, and lives, particularly if they're held in solitary confinement. In extreme cases, defendants may have their cases severed from their codefendants' cases, or put on hold pending competency hearings; defendants may also be under pressure to take plea agreements to avoid institutionalization and competency hearings. Prosecutors often try to use any documented mental health history against radicals in pretrial and trial hearings, such as arguing for high bail or no bail, discussing their radical politics as mental illness, and arguing for sentencing enhancements because they are a threat to society. Additionally, prisoners with mental health needs often receive writeups for disciplinary infractions and/or are placed in solitary confinement, which can make their mental health worse and put them at greater risk of harm. Attorneys are often the only people who have access to regular contact with prisoners with mental health needs, and are thus well positioned to monitor or understand how a defendant's mental health might be deteriorating over time. Thus, attorneys representing radicals with these needs can work with their client's defense committee, other supporters, and loved ones to support them.

The Icarus Project offers many resources, including publications and webinars. The National Alliance on Mental Illness (NAMI) offers a number of resources for people living with mental illness and their loved ones, including a helpline (1-800-950-NAMI) and a series of videos about supporting and advocating for these prisoners. There may also be federal, state, or local governmental or nongovernmental resources available.

2.8 Physical Health Needs

Many prisoners need medications or have acute or

chronic medical needs, including disabilities, which require immediate or constant attention. This can be something as seemingly simple as needing a pair of glasses, or something as complicated as needing lifesaving medication on a daily basis. This attention is routinely denied in jail and prison, often putting prisoners at great risk, leading to irreversible medical conditions, or causing death. As with other situations that put prisoners in vulnerable positions, prosecutors may use these healthcare needs to try to force plea agreements or cooperation, and guards may use those needs to single-out and abuse prisoners. Attorneys may be able to work with the defendant's defense committee, other supporters, or loved ones to persuade the jail to provide the defendant with the necessary healthcare and access to medications.

Resources to explore include The Arc's initiative on criminal justice, the Disability Rights Bar Association, and the Judge David L. Bazelon Center for Mental Health Law. There may also be federal, state, or local governmental or nongovernmental resources available. Many of the situations that prisoners with these needs face may be Eighth Amendment issues, and there may be specific legal remedies to change the conditions of their imprisonment.

3.0 Thoughts on Compensation

In this section, we address attorneys who represent radical defendants as part of their own political commitments, and who can vary the fees for their legal services. Our thoughts on compensation may also be of interest to attorneys who are new to representing radicals and are inspired by their political or ideological commitments and sacrifices. These thoughts might be interesting to other lawyers representing radicals, but are not likely to be applicable (i.e., when the court sets the rate for representation).

Even when lawyers can offer representation *pro bono* or "*low bono*" (i.e., significantly reduced legal fees), their expenses need to be met. Many radical attorneys recommend clearly outlining the costs of representation in the representation agreement. This part of the agreement could specify that the money paid to the lawyer will be a flat fee no matter the duration of the case, a set fee for pretrial proceedings and a reduced hourly rate if the case goes to trial, an understanding that paying the fees may take months or years of fundraising rather than being paid as billed, or whatever agreement makes sense for the individual circumstance. Radical clients' access to financial resources can vary greatly, but many are situationally or generationally poor and live in precarity; thus, consideration by both attorney and client of the financial landscape may be a useful part of determining what fees are amenable to everyone. If your jurisdiction allows for nontraditional compensation arrangements, you might be able to create an agreement that includes trading goods or services, work-trade for investigative or administrative services on future cases, et cetera. This type of agreement is not without precedent; many movement attorneys have prided themselves on charging little to no fee for services.[4]

Whatever agreement is reached, outlining the expenses

the lawyer anticipates (e.g., their time, court fees, office supplies, travel) when creating a representation agreement can help prevent conflict over money in the future. Likewise, clearly outlining the expenses the client (and the defense committee, if applicable) anticipates (e.g., travel for the client and supporters, publicity materials, bookkeeping, web hosting, rent, food) and the funds they think they may realistically be able to raise can help the attorney understand the financial constraints their client is likely to face throughout the case.

Over the years, many movement attorneys who have received large amounts of money for their criminal defense of radical clients have donated a portion of those fees to other cases or to political organizations as part of their contributions to radical movements. Other lawyers have accepted less than the original amount agreed on, such as when their financial situation allowed them to waive fees if clients facing financial hardships were unable to pay the agreed-upon amount. Whether agreements like this are put in place or not, lawyers representing radicals can consider ways of sharing funds forward to help support radical movements in a broader way. This often entails lawyers reflecting on their own financial situations, class backgrounds, access to resources, and individual needs in comparison with the situations of their clients and the communities these clients come from.

Unfortunately, the point also needs to be made that money should never be used as power within relationships between attorneys and radical clients. There have been times when attorneys representing radicals have provided low-quality representation because the case was *pro bono* or *low bono*, have threatened to not file motions until they were paid (or intimated that this was the case), have demanded more money than agreed upon when large amounts of money were fundraised for the client's support, or have threatened to sue over remaining funds raised by the defense committee. These regrettable instances are by no means common, but they are tragic and can be part of long-lasting fractures within radical communities and can cause mistrust of attorneys. Coming to clear agreements on money at the outset of cases can hopefully reduce the chances of money becoming an issue at any point.

Chapter 4: Working with Political Support

1.0 What Is a Defense Committee?

Defense committees and other forms of political support have served an important political purpose throughout US history. An early example is the Amistad Committee, which was composed of slavery abolitionists who supported a slave revolt on a Spanish ship, *La Amistad*.[1] Over the decades since then, friends, family, and fellow community members of radical clients have organized support efforts for them; the names and organizational structures of these efforts vary and can include defense committee, support crew, antirepression committee, legal collective, et cetera. Additionally, there are also organizing models such as participatory defense that are working to create structures to support people from oppressed communities facing charges. Whatever form these support structures take or whatever they call themselves, they can help clients be better positioned to fully explore their legal options and goals with their attorney, which is typically the realm of the attorney-client relationship. As we discuss in this chapter, defense committee organizing and legal defenses can be complementary efforts. We generally use "defense committee" as shorthand for any support effort for defendants.

The structures and degrees of formality that defense committees assume can vary, often depending on client needs and desires or on the values, priorities, and capacity of committee members. In general, defense committees have worked most effectively when clients are actively involved in their formation, goals, decisions about tactics and strategies for building solidarity and applying political pressure, and decisions about important support matters (e.g., money, Internet or social media platforms used, types of media creation, et cetera). This client involvement is even more complicated when defendants are incarcerated for all or part of their pretrial process, as well as when they must serve jail/prison sentences. Even with these obstacles, however, defense committees typically operate most effectively when they are aligned with defendants' wishes. Attorneys representing radicals should understand not only the benefit of defense committees for the defendants, but also the ways in which defense committees can help clients make the best decisions about their cases.

Although defense committees may exist only during pretrial proceedings and dissolve if the people facing charges are acquitted or the charges are dropped, some exist for several years while the accused face charges and serve their sentences, and some exist for decades to help prisoners through long sentences and/or to fight for their release. Likewise, a defense committee may be highly organized and official (e.g., having nonprofit status, a business bank account and other nonprofit financial structures, a board of directors, et cetera). Others are less formal groupings or networks of people who have come together to support radicals from particular movements but do not coordinate directly with each other. Legal collectives (also called "law collectives") or antirepression committees may already be active within a particular community and can serve the role as a defense committee for new cases, as well. Finally—and importantly—many times the work that defense committees typically do is done by family members or loved ones of incarcerated persons, such as mothers, grandmothers, or partners.

Defense committees typically take on many areas of organizing to demonstrate solidarity with defendants. These can include political pressure campaigns, fundraising, media, propaganda, assisting with the legal defense in ways that support the attorney-client relationship, and direct prisoner support during incarceration. Most defense committees also help defendants with their life needs, such as housing, travel, and childcare. Likewise, most help them with weathering the emotional ups and downs of their legal proceedings. Defense committees can also function as a sounding board for radicals as they define and refine their political strategies and weigh their legal options.

Some defense committees may also extend solidarity and logistical support to other people in the defendant's life who may be adversely affected by the criminal charges or convictions (e.g., partners, children or other dependents, et cetera).

2.0 How Defense Committees Can Benefit Clients and Attorneys

Attorneys who are unfamiliar with defense committees may consider them to be interference in the attorney-client relationship, a threat to confidentiality, or irrelevant to the legal situation at hand. There are several obvious considerations about protecting privileged conversations and client confidentiality that radical clients, like most clients, often need to be instructed on. Nevertheless, there are many reasons for attorneys to be glad their clients have a defense committee and to find ways to balance the needs of the legal defense with the personal and political support that defense committees can provide.

2.1 Helping Clients Set and Focus on Legal Goals

Defense committees can help defendants fully explore and understand their legal options in ways that are complementary to the attorney's work and legal advice. Many times, people who have faced charges themselves, have been convicted previously, and/or have been incarcerated previously are involved in defense committees. These people can provide clients with invaluable insight into their situations, the potential positive or negative consequences of their legal decisions, and the personal and political ramifications of particular choices. Many of these people are skilled in discussing legal options without discussing the facts of a case, and will generally prioritize finding successful ways of helping the accused make choices without damaging their legal defense.

Additionally, lawyers are often able to coordinate with a defense committee to ensure attorney-client privilege is being maintained while their client is receiving solid, well-rounded support. That support may look like social visits while in jail or on house arrest pretrial during which they talk about the personal and political ramifications of legal decisions. Lawyers can help ensure these situations are navigated effectively by clearly communicating to their clients and the defense committee what can and should not be discussed between the defendant and anyone other than their lawyer.

2.2 Supporting the Legal Strategy

Defense committees may also be able to help with the legal strategy aspects of the case. For example, some members of the defense committee or other supporters might be able to help dig through discovery under attorney supervision, make public records requests, serve subpoenas, or help with legal research. (In some cases, radicals working as paralegals under attorney supervision have helped with writing motions as well.) These collaborations can also go a long way towards reducing costs and saving time. Additionally, the defense committee may know or be able to track down potential witnesses who might have otherwise been unknown or unreachable. They also might have access to information and communities that the attorneys do not, which can open new avenues for legal strategy.[2] For example, if there is an informant in the case, defense committee members might know people unrelated to the case who know the informant from other situations and could provide invaluable information about them.

Defense committees can also create and coordinate infrastructure to take court notes at pretrial hearings, trial, and postconviction relief/appeal hearings. For example, volunteers could take shifts taking detailed notes on the public portion of hearings. These notes can then be shared with radical clients and their attorneys after court to help jog their memories about what transpired until official transcripts are obtained or as a surrogate for notes that a legal assistant would take. Additionally, these notes can help defense committees with media work when it is part of the political support strategy (see Section 4.0 in this chapter and chapter 5). These notes can also record aspects of the court proceedings that transcripts do not capture, such as nonverbal reactions from the judge and jury.

2.2.1 Legal Liaisons

We want to highlight an organizing model that is seldom considered in political cases: the legal liaison. Many attorneys, radical clients, and defense committee members have found it helpful to have a legal liaison within the defense committee who can be responsible for communicating with the attorney so they can use their time efficiently rather than needing to respond to multiple people, have the same conversation multiple times, et cetera. The liaison is usually a member of the defense committee who serves as the bridge between the legal team and the defense committee and other supporters. When supporters come to court hearings, they often have many questions, concerns, and fears about what will happen next and what the judge's rulings meant. The liaison can help answer questions in the moment and follow-up with you after court to get clarification and help ensure your client also fully understands everything that happened in court. This model can also be effective when family members and loved ones are involved in the defense committee, as they often have distinct areas of concern that benefit from close coordination with attorneys. Legal liaisons can thus support lawyers with in-depth, time-intensive communication with the client's loved ones so that lawyers are not overwhelmed with those needs in addition to their client's urgent legal needs.

Legal liaisons can also be helpful if you are not familiar with your client's ideological framework. Liaisons can be well positioned to help you understand the political nature of the case, where your client is coming from and what their goals are, and why so many people are interested in the case. Similarly, they can help you with communication and coordination with your client and their loved ones, particularly when legal proceedings become confusing, scary, or simply long and exhausting.

2.3 Providing Financial Support

Defense committees can help raise money for your client's defense expenses as well as their ongoing support while fighting their charges. Many radical clients rely on a defense committee for raising money, as they often do not have substantial means of their own or access to financial resources. Fundraising campaigns for clear, direct asks (e.g., money for an investigator, money for court transcripts) can be relatively easy to develop and run, which can expand the range of possible legal options for your client.

2.4 Drawing Attention to Repression

Defense committees can also conduct political and/or media campaigns that neither the attorney nor the clients can undertake themselves. For example, a district attorney up for re-election who has environmental justice as part of their political platform but is vehemently prosecuting pipeline protesters may face political consequences if the defense committee makes the public aware of the repressive nature of the prosecutions. The defense committee can make that case with the public, whereas it may be a dead end in the courtroom or inappropriate for the lawyer to make in a venue outside of the courtroom. The defense committee can also use creative humor or satire in its defense of the politics of the case, which could backfire if the attorney or client tried it.

Parallel Strategies: The Case of Louis Hunter
by Tim Phillips, Esq.

On July 9, 2016, there was a large protest in St. Paul, MN, in response to the murder of Philando Castile by a police officer. The demonstration temporarily shut down traffic on I-94, and many protesters threw objects at police. Following the protest, Louis Hunter, a second cousin of Castile, was arrested and charged with two counts of felony riot. Hunter allegedly threw rocks, construction debris, and Molotov cocktails at officers. He was the only person charged with a felony, although others were charged with misdemeanor counts of refusing to disperse.

I represented Hunter and focused on the legal strategy. Simultaneously, local anarchists organized support alongside Hunter and his community. Together, they organized press conferences, court support, call-in days, and fundraisers, as well as a collective defense strategy that involved the dozens of people arrested at various protests against police violence in the Twin Cities following Castile's death. The defense committee's goals included telling Hunter's story as another example of state violence against Black people, helping him pay the bills in the aftermath of his arrest, and getting his charges dropped.

As a result of this organizing, dozens of people arrested at various protests against police violence in the Twin Cities refused to take any plea deals until Hunter's charges were dropped. The first trial group said they were going to trial in solidarity with Hunter; the week before their trial, his charges were dismissed due to "insufficient evidence." Organizing around Hunter's case absolutely contributed to this legal victory and strengthened broader movements against police violence and white supremacy.

It should be stressed here that defense committees should avoid building support for the defendants based solely on appeals to the defendant's innocence. "**Innocence politics**" are not helpful to larger political movements, and can be confusing to supporters if the case is eventually resolved through a plea.

In many political cases over the years, defense committees, clients, and lawyers have worked in close coordination to address all aspects of the cases and the clients' various goals and priorities for their cases. These collaborations and complementary efforts were possible even when the types of tasks they completed were drastically different (e.g., privileged discussions about legal strategy versus press conferences or public demonstrations).

2.5 Providing Personal Support for Radical Clients

Perhaps most importantly, defense committees can help your client feel resilient and connected to the outside world during a difficult and stressful time. The criminal legal system is designed to break people down so they feel isolated and powerless, so this connection with supporters can go a long way towards helping them maintain their physical, emotional, and mental health. As you have likely seen with other clients, this support helps them stay emotionally and mentally present to deal with their case as the two of you fight the charges together.

This personal support can take many forms. It may encompass one-on-one support with day-to-day living, arranging entertaining group activities such as movie nights, and/or creating space for deep, personal conversations about their fears regarding facing charges. Additionally, if your client is in custody pretrial, a defense committee can ensure they receive regular visits, send them letters and books, and keep money on their commissary. All these efforts can go a long way towards helping them survive their ordeals and be better prepared to strive for their personal, political, and legal goals.

2.5.1 Supporting the Most Vulnerable Clients

We would be remiss not to address the brutal reality that the criminal legal system is designed to harm people and is especially effective at doing this to those who were vulnerable or in precarious situations before they entered the system. Not only are interactions with police officers often life-or-death situations for many people, but being mired in intense legal situations can be as well. Defense committees can provide direct support for incarcerated radicals in ways that are explicitly about saving the person's life.

Further, clients who are not well connected in radical movements or in their local communities may feel isolated or receive little support from people who don't know them personally. Similarly, clients who were entrapped by government agents or informants are often distanced from friends and comrades by the informant throughout the course of the entrapment effort, so they may experience more isolation than if the informant had never targeted them. People who knew the arrestees but were not prey to the informant's tactics may also feel scared and be reluctant to put themselves on the government's radar by directly supporting the defendants, which weakens political movements in general and often leaves defendants even more vulnerable.

Defendants who feel isolated and vulnerable are seldom in good positions to make the best decisions for themselves. On a political level, they can also be more susceptible to betraying their comrades and their own principles when pressured by the prosecution to cooperate against others. Defense committees can help defendants in these situations deal with the stress and fear produced by their situations, as well as to make the best decisions for themselves and their movements.

These realities highlight not only how important it can be for defense committees to be active and in close touch with defendants, but also why their attorneys should welcome and encourage strong, cohesive defense committees.

3.0 How Attorneys Can Benefit Radicals and Defense Committees

In addition to all the ethical obligations that are covered in law school and the skills lawyers learn on the job while interacting with their clients, representing radical clients presents particular opportunities that might be unfamiliar or at least uncommon to some lawyers. Chapter 3 covers these situations in depth. In terms of engaging with defense committees, there are many ways that attorneys can benefit their clients as well as their defense committees and political movements.

Collaborating With a Defense Committee
by Mark Vermeulen, Esq. and Ben Rosenfeld, Esq.

Eric McDavid's case is an especially egregious example of state repression against anarchist environmentalists. His defense committee, Sacramento Prisoner Support (SPS), provided him with day-to-day support, engaged in political organizing, and assisted his legal team throughout his pretrial incarceration, trial, and prison sentence.

After Eric received an outrageous sentence of almost twenty years in prison, members of SPS filed a Freedom of Information Act (FOIA) request and skillfully assisted our habeas legal team with researching and drafting the habeas petition we filed in May 2012. This petition and the evidence uncovered through FOIA led to Eric's release from prison more than a decade early.

Without their support, hard work, and dedication, it is almost certain that Eric would still be in prison today. Our legal success was a result of the collaboration between his legal supporters and his lawyers, which was mutually sought and welcomed by Eric and his team, with his best interests at heart.

3.1 Providing Radicals With the Best Representation

Clients who approach their cases with a view towards more than strictly legal goals and priorities often value having defense committees and see them as a crucial part of their overall defense effort. In this sense, attorneys working with defense committees can view this role as part of their efforts to provide their clients with the best possible defense. Working with defense committees and supporting their efforts can thus be seen as complementary to the typical components of representation.

3.2 Balancing Political and Legal Strategies

Although the degree of collaboration and mutual support between attorneys and defense committees can vary greatly, agreeing on some measure of collaboration can be beneficial. In many political cases over the years, attorneys have assisted defense committees with certain strategic decisions, such as media (e.g., talking points, press releases, coordinating around important court dates), publicity (e.g., propaganda, language used in fundraising appeals), and pressure campaigns (e.g., protesting district attorneys at their re-election campaign events).

Additionally, the defense committee may want to seek your advice on specific details or considerations to ensure they do not inadvertently damage or complicate the developing legal strategy, which the committee may not have any more insight into than any other spectator at a public hearing. The ins and outs of what is appropriate or acceptable coordination can vary greatly by the jurisdiction or the court, as well as the comfort level of everyone involved in the defense effort, so there is no one best way of figuring out how to balance political and legal strategies, priorities, and goals. Nonetheless, there is often more room to figure out workable, mutually beneficial relationships than may be apparent at first.

One example of an effective balance between political and legal strategy can been seen in the case of CeCe Mc-Donald, a Black trans woman who was charged with two counts of murder after surviving a racist, transphobic attack in 2011 during which her attacker, a **cisgender** white man, was stabbed and bled to death. The legal strategy in this case was to pursue a self-defense argument. Although some media outlets advanced a self-defense argument on their own, the defense committee's political pressure campaign instead highlighted the racism and transphobia embedded in the county attorney's office as a way to pressure the prosecutor to drop the charges. This political strategy worked in tandem with the legal strategy to add nuance to the media conversation about the case without advancing narratives that could be construed as a legal defense, or later coming into conflict with the legal defense as it developed throughout the case. Specifically, the defense committee was careful not to talk about the facts of the case or any actions McDonald may or may not have taken, instead focusing on the political significance of a Black trans woman being attacked because of her racial and gender identity. This political campaign was designed to put pressure on the prosecutor to drop the charges because he prided himself on being an "LGBTQ-friendly" prosecutor and spoke publicly about his efforts to eliminate homophobia in his office.

The robust legal defense from the legal team and vibrant political pressure campaign from the defense committee were both aided by media coverage on the eve of trial that highlighted McDonald's case and cast an unfavorable light on the county attorney's office. Ultimately, McDonald was offered a plea agreement during jury selection that reduced her prison time from a maximum of forty years to only a few years on top of the time she had already served.

The legal team and defense committee worked together effectively in McDonald's case, and the benefits to her ended up being measurable in terms of the decades in prison she was no longer facing. Even when there is less coordination and communication between the legal team and defense committee, it is still possible for both teams to play their respective roles in complementary ways that ultimately benefit people facing charges and center their wishes.

3.3 Demystifying the Legal System

Another role that attorneys might find themselves being asked to play, or that they might want to play as part of their political support for movements, is to help educate supporters about what is happening in the client's case and in court. The criminal legal system and the implications of motions, arguments, and court decisions are often mystifying to supporters. Although this educational role might seem like a daunting, time-consuming task, many lawyers representing radicals have found it to be rewarding and beneficial to work well with their clients.

Talking with supporters after court hearings to help explain what just happened could be a crucial part of facilitating this education and establishing healthy ties with the defense committee. As mentioned earlier, a legal liaison can help with this role so it's not overwhelming. Sharing filed motions (both your own and the prosecution's) with the defense committee can be another aspect of this education. Although some lawyers may want to withhold motions and orders because of the sensitive information often contained in them, taking an educational approach to addressing these public documents can be more beneficial than leaving it up to reporters to put their own spin on them or to wait for the prosecution to feed their perspectives to the media as incontrovertible truths. Thus, sharing public documents with the defense committee can help it mount political and media campaigns in ways that do not damage or complicate your client's legal defense. Tactical and strategic decisions about how to leverage these documents—or not—are often best decided collaboratively with the client and their defense committee.

Similarly, many defense committees want to post court documents on the political support website to help educate other radicals about ways in which the government is using particular criminal charges to repress their political movements. At times, attorneys, clients, and defense committee members may disagree on the wisdom and strategic value of posting these documents, even though those that are not under seal are public documents accessible by anyone—including adversarial reporters and people who view radical social movements as their enemies. Court documents can often be viewed as tools with varying amounts of tactical and strategic significance in the political realm in addition to the legal record being developed. Attorneys can help defense committees understand the significance of court documents and figure out how to use or not use them in the political realm; this is a common crossover between balancing a client's political and legal goals and the attorney demystifying the criminal legal system.

By helping to educate their client and supporters at

every step of the criminal legal process, attorneys act in solidarity with movements and support effective political organizing. Because laws and legal proceedings are often intentionally obfuscated, you can serve an important function for movements by demystifying the process and using court documents in ways that aid your client and their movements.

Attorney-Client Privilege and the Advantages of Open Communication
by Michael Deutsch, Esq., People's Law Office (PLO)

The founding principle of the People's Law Office was to use our legal skills to empower our clients. In our defense of political activists, we believe it is of critical importance to carefully review with our clients the legal procedures and options at each stage of their case, jointly discuss legal strategies, and make collective decisions. This requires open communication with our clients every step of the way.

We implemented the strategy of amnesty for the rebelling Attica prisoners, and sought to jail Governor Nelson Rockefeller, who ordered the massacre, as well as the state police and prison guards who carried it out. In our defense of Puerto Rican *independentistas* (independence fighters) charged with seditious conspiracy, we supported their political position to assert **prisoners of war** status, desire not to participate in their criminal cases, and refusal to recognize the US court's right to criminalize their resistance to US colonialism. We brought petitions before international tribunals asserting their rights under international law. In representing Palestinians falsely accused of terrorism, we presented to the court and jury the systematic torture and denial of human rights for our clients by the Israeli government.

We understand that it is a priority to work closely with our political clients' supporters and communities, even when this means navigating around tough issues of attorney-client privilege and communication with supporters. We meet after each court appearance to explain to courtrooms filled with supporters what took place. We also freely give our time to speak at community events and write about the cases. In many cases, the presence of supporters in the courtroom and our public educational work made a significant difference in the outcome.

4.0 Defense Committees and the Media

We have already touched a bit on media as a common part of politically motivated cases against radicals, and we explore this topic in depth in chapter 5. Yet a few brief points merit attention here.

Often, lawyers and clients, and/or lawyers and defense committees, have drastically different ideas of whether engaging with the media is a good idea or not, much less how doing so is most effective and strategic. Decisions about whether to engage with the media are specific to each situation, so we will not attempt to provide a rule or rubric on them. However, everyone involved will invariably benefit from having clear, direct conversations about these decisions.

In most criminal cases, the legal situation changes as the case advances towards trial, during the trial itself, in between conviction and sentencing, and after sentencing. As such, having conversations about media tactics and strategies can be beneficial in advance or at the beginning of each stage in the life of a criminal case. Decisions made about media outlets or strategy in one stage do not necessarily need to be maintained at subsequent stages, although actions taken or not taken in the past obviously have repercussions on future decisions. Nevertheless, media strategy is as fluid as legal strategy and is best addressed on a regular basis in a well-considered way with the broader goals and situation in mind.

5.0 Common Challenges

There is a range of common challenging situations involving defense committees that warrants discussion. Many of these situations are part of typical criminal cases as well, although they may manifest differently or present frustrations or obstacles that are not usually experienced in typical criminal cases.

5.1 Legal

Although defense committees are not generally covered by attorney-client privilege, there are several common scenarios in which they can help radical clients make their legal decisions and help lawyers with various logistical matters. There are also ways for members of defense committees to work under the supervision of attorneys, although what is possible may vary by jurisdiction.

5.1.1 Multiple Defendants

When there are multiple defendants in one case, a defense committee for all the defendants together may be the most desirable or feasible arrangement. The benefits of this support structure are often that it helps defendants maintain solidarity and gives them a forum in which to discuss any disagreements about their legal strategies and decisions. Of course, this collaboration cannot totally prevent individual defendants' legal interests from conflicting with their codefendants' interests; likewise, it cannot prevent people from having disagreements or interpersonal conflicts.

Nevertheless, if defendants get into personal or political conflicts, the defense committee may be able to help them work through those conflicts. The defense committee may also be in a good position to help the defendants have productive conversations about how to make their individual legal choices and develop their individual defense strategies through privileged conversations with their attorneys in ways that help all of them pursue all their goals without harming each other. In these ways, defense committees can help defendants participate most effectively in developing their legal strategies and making decisions with their attorneys.

5.1.2 Witnesses

Because liberatory political movements value personal relationships, collaborative efforts, and interdependence, there may be people who could be potential defense witnesses in the case who might be inclined to become members of defense committees, spokespeople in media campaigns, attendees at court hearings, or otherwise deeply involved in the political aspects of cases. These potential witnesses would benefit not only from understanding how their support efforts could positively or negatively affect their value as witnesses for your client, but also from securing their own counsel. Many times, people who could be witnesses may be invested in being able to provide the best testimony even if there are implications for how they engage in support efforts. Knowing when it is more beneficial to serve as a witness than a defense committee member is not intuitive, however, and frank discussions and education about the legal nuances for your jurisdiction are often important.

Additionally, there may be members of the defense committee who are subpoenaed by the prosecution and thus should not have direct contact with the defendants. Not having direct contact with defense committee members or others close to the defendants is also often sensible, as no one will want to provide the prosecutor with an opportunity to claim witness tampering or harassment, for example. People in this situation might not understand the complexities that come with being subpoenaed to testify against a friend, and thus education about this situation can help everyone protect the defendant's legal case.

5.2 Political

At times, radical clients view their political goals as more important than the legal outcome of their charges. Clients with these priorities often want their defense committees to be active in mounting a political defense and building solidarity for them, which can at times present challenges for attorneys who are accustomed to traditional approaches to legal defense. Considerations for how to represent radical clients with these priorities are explored in depth in chapter 3.

In terms of defense committees, attorneys who are challenged by their client's adherence to political goals and strategies would likely benefit from understanding defense committees as a way in which their client is getting what they want out of an otherwise terrible experience, not as an obstacle to attorneys representing their clients. As a lawyer representing radicals, it can be important to advise your client and their defense committee to avoid pursuing political goals based solely on notions of innocence, especially because the case may be settled with a guilty plea. Avoiding this political pitfall will not only best support your client, but will offer a sound political framework for future organizing.

5.3 Interpersonal

Defense committees are often well positioned to help clients navigate interpersonal situations. What follows are considerations for interpersonal scenarios that commonly lead to tension within cases against radicals.

5.3.1 Families and Loved Ones

Families (biological, adopted, or chosen) and loved ones of radical clients often want to actively support them. At times, these support efforts are incorporated into defense committee efforts; at other times, they are separate. Although different groups working together is often best for everyone involved, families and defense committees are able to better support the needs of the person facing charges when they take on separate roles in their support.

As the attorney, you can ask the defense committee

and the family and/or loved ones to figure things out between themselves and not involve you in inappropriate or counterproductive ways. As explored earlier, a legal liaison can be effective in such situations.

5.3.2 Conflict Within Defense Committees

There may at times be conflict within defense committees. This conflict can often add to the stress that radicals facing charges experience, especially if they are incarcerated pretrial. This conflict can also spill out into a defense committee's interactions with the attorney. As the attorney, it can be appropriate for you to set clear boundaries about when and how you will handle these conflicts or complex situations.

Conflict within a defense committee is not inherently negative. Conflict can transform the defense committee's goals, structure, or strategy in ways that benefit your client. For example, a defense committee may decide to shift the political goals or tactics as a result of internal dialogue, or divide its task load based on internal preferences and skill sets (e.g., some people primarily create media, others provide emotional and direct support, others do court support, et cetera).

5.4 Money

Because defense committees often take on fundraising for defense and support efforts, it can be easy for people to assume there will be money for every conceivable need, or that they are entitled to money because it was raised. The reality is that hard decisions about how to spend limited resources often have to be made on a regular basis while keeping the long view in mind. This can mean that there is effectively little money for any given expenditure, including legal fees, even if the dollar amount raised appears to be large.

Further, defense committees often find that fundraising is easier at certain stages of cases than others. For example, it is often relatively easy to raise money immediately after arrests and significantly harder when people are serving many years or decades in prison. Experienced defense committees may thus be particularly cautious about financial decisions and prioritize stretching funds over making decisions with the assumption that there will always be more money. A well-organized defense committee may publicize the purposes of funds at the outset of their fundraising efforts (e.g., legal defense, rent, publicity materials, web hosting expenses, et cetera) to increase transparency about monetary decisions. However, many efforts are figured out during crisis when everyone involved is doing this work for the first time. The level of organization of the fundraising apparatus, including whether efforts are organized as registered nonprofits or not, can vary drastically, as can the level of shared understanding of what funds are available for and when.

A final point needs to be made: Many members of defense committees consider funds raised for particular cases to be funds for *movement support* rather than for the individual named defendants in cases. The difference is often in seeing money raised as *resources to support anyone targeted by the government* versus *resources for these particular defendants*. It is important for fundraising efforts enacted in support of defendants to be explicit about this from the outset.

One implication of this distinction is that radicals and defense committees may view raised funds as pooled resources that can be directed elsewhere when the situation at hand no longer requires financial support. This position contrasts with viewing the funds as an organizational budget that should be spent down to close out an organization. Another implication is that funds are often viewed as resources to benefit movements as a whole, in contrast to discretionary funds for individuals to spend as they wish. Similarly, funds set aside to be stretched out over years or decades of incarceration can be viewed as necessary resources for fighting back against the systemic oppression of the prison-industrial complex, and thus a way of following through on the broader political movement's responsibilities to those who are targeted. In this way, funds are often viewed as necessary components of sustained political struggle rather than a budget for a particular criminal case.

As an attorney representing a radical client, it is important to understand how money is being considered and managed by defense committees and defendants. Creating clear representation agreements that specify timelines and amounts of payment for attorney's fees and other legal costs can go a long way towards ensuring that money does not become a source of conflict.

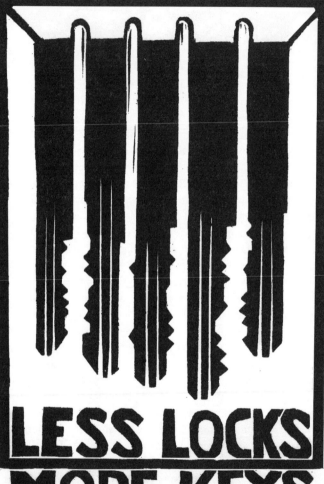

**LESS LOCKS
MORE KEYS**

Chapter 5: Engaging with the Media

Chapter Outline

1.0 Media and Social Media in Cases against Radicals

Media and social media are two common areas of misunderstanding, conflicting priorities and goals, and disagreement between attorneys and radical clients. Many times, defense attorneys are wary of any media attention and opposed to their clients making public appearances while charges are pending. Other times, attorneys might approach the media at strategic moments to complement legal strategies. Whatever the situation, clients and attorneys may or may not agree on priorities and strategies.

This chapter explores the common tensions between attorneys and radical clients regarding media and social media, as well as between attorneys and defense committees. Radicals facing charges and their defense committees likely have diverse thoughts on the pros and cons of engaging with the media and/or using social media, so we do not try to provide a handbook for using media in criminal cases. Rather, we hope to help attorneys work with their

Confidentiality and Security Culture Under Global Digital Surveillance
by Michele Gretes, Civil Liberties Defense Center (CLDC) Digital Security Program

Unchecked digital surveillance by governments and powerful corporations places radicals and their social movements at a serious disadvantage. Huge volumes of passively collected communications help the government suppress activists and anticipate their actions. Prosecutors can also use this data in the parallel construction of cases using *post hoc*, legally gathered evidence.

The right to remain silent is seriously undermined by information recovered from seized devices, or by email or text messages obtained from service providers. Fortunately, strong encryption is increasingly available and easier to use. Consider these four key steps:

1. Use open-source, *end-to-end encrypted* platforms to keep your messages, calls, and documents private. The keys used to decipher data never leave activists' or attorneys' devices. At the time of writing, easy and powerful options are: Signal (simple individual and group messaging and one-on-one voice/video calls), Wire (messaging and audio calls for up to ten devices), Keybase (encrypted team messaging and shared file storage), and Cryptpad (shared document creation). Whenever possible, set messages to disappear after a reasonable amount of time. For group video or big calls, consider using Jitsi Meet—this isn't end-to-end encrypted but, so long as you can trust the host (e.g., meet.mayfirst.org), it's the best current option.

2. Protect your devices with regular *security updates and encrypted storage*. Use as long and random a passcode as possible (numbers, letters, symbols) and disable fingerprint or face unlocking. iPhones should be set to erase data after ten failed passcode attempts. For laptops, encrypt disks using FileVault (Mac/OSX), VeraCrypt (Windows), or LUKS (Linux). A disk encryption passphrase of six randomly chosen words is both memorable and unbreakable. Power down (not just sleep) computers when at risk of seizure.

3. Keep online accounts under your control by using a reputable *password manager* (e.g., Bitwarden, KeePassXC, or 1Password, plus that six-word passphrase) to assign unique passwords for each account. Use *two-step (multifactor) authentication* codes generated by an app instead of text message whenever possible.

4. Keep important relationships *off social media* as much as possible (at minimum, don't make conversations and friend lists public) to make it harder for police and prosecutors to map activist networks. Likewise, some messaging platforms (like Signal or Briar) take steps to protect *metadata* (who you're contacting, when, and how often). Tor Browser or a paid, non–US-based VPN can anonymize web browsing when doing research online.

clients and defense committees to make strategic decisions about media that support their client's goals without jeopardizing broader social struggles or exposing radicals to further digital surveillance.

The remainder of this section explores the common types of media that are often in play in political cases. Mainstream media, independent media, **movement media**, and social media all have their own advantages and disadvantages.

1.1 Mainstream Media

Mainstream media encompasses media outlets such as network news (e.g., Fox, NBC), local and national newspapers/news magazines (e.g., *USA Today*, *Time*, *New York Times*), news/political commentary programs on major networks, and network radio programs (e.g., *The Rush Limbaugh Show*). Mainstream media will likely not hesitate to vilify your client, their comrades, and their movements. They may capitalize on your client's race, gender, mental health, and arrest history to demonize them and their supporters. These outlets typically rely on the police and the prosecutors to feed them stories and leak documents, so engaging with them can be challenging and dangerous. However, your client may wish to engage with mainstream media if it affords them an opportunity to challenge the narrative being put forth about their case and/or to highlight the broader social and political issues surrounding their criminal charges.

1.2 Independent Media

Leftist independent media can often be more sympathetic to your client, their case, and the broader movements of which they may be a part (e.g., *Democracy Now!*, *The Intercept*). They usually have a broader reach than movement media, and cultivating relationships with these outlets and freelance journalists can have substantial positive impacts on your client's case. However, this does not mean that they will always act in your client's best interest. Your client is not their priority—getting their story out, making a name for themselves, or producing original content is more likely to be their top priority. Your client should be advised to choose their media engagement carefully based on their broader political and legal goals.

1.3 Movement Media

Movement media (or "resistance media") is media created by and for radicals. The individuals and collectives who run these media outlets (websites, podcasts, radio shows, magazines, et cetera) will generally be the most willing to help your client. Some examples of movement media include: SubMedia (a video collective), *It's Going Down* (a news site), Unicorn Riot (a media collective), and *The Final Straw* (a radio show). Movement media has the advantage of reaching an audience nationally and internationally that will almost certainly be willing to support radical clients (through fundraising, educational events, rallies, and other

political efforts). When radical clients want media attention brought to their cases, receiving coverage in these outlets can often help them feel support and solidarity in ways
that other media coverage will not.

A potential limitation of movement media is that most
of the audience may already be inclined to support your
client and thus the coverage may simply be "preaching to
the choir." Another potential drawback is that these media
outlets might have goals or agendas that come into conflict
with the defendant's goals for their case. For example, they
might want to portray your client as an uncompromising
warrior for animal liberation when your client plans to use
an entrapment defense at trial to assert how an undercover
operative coerced them into taking an illegal action.

1.4 Social Media

No chapter on media would be complete without
thoughts on social media (Facebook, Twitter, Instagram,
SnapChat, et cetera). These platforms are routinely used as
a form of surveillance by governmental departments such as
Homeland Security and ICE, local police, and private security firms. Social media companies also profit by providing
data about their users to an increasing number of data min-
ing companies that can use this data in an almost limitless
number of ways. As legal workers who have repeatedly seen
social media used against radicals and movements in devastating ways, we believe that the most security-conscious approach is to not use social media at all, either personally or

politically. However, we realize that people will continue using social media, so we must address some ways to mitigate its harmful effects. A thorough examination of this topic is outside the scope of this book, as is a functional guide to reducing the risks inherent to social media. We recommend the Electronic Frontier Foundation as a resource for understanding and navigating the risks of using social media.

The potential liabilities of social media to individuals and social movements is increasingly well documented. The wealth of data that social media apps and smartphones make available to law enforcement, private security firms, and third parties effectively hands over information to these entities that they would otherwise have to spend significant investigative resources to obtain. Using social media also provides the government with information on how to conduct their investigation more effectively, such as who to interview (and where to find them), as well as plenty of audio and video recordings, textual records, and location data to use against people in legal proceedings.

Because of these pitfalls, our advice for defendants is that they deactivate all their personal social media accounts as soon as possible after being charged, or if they anticipate charges or grand jury subpoenas being imposed on them in the future. These steps are often only capable of mitigating harm or preventing future harm, as any data collected prior to deactivation may have already been obtained and search warrants of accounts will provide the government with most or all of that data anyway. Nevertheless, deactivating social media accounts immediately may help reduce the likelihood of further dangerous or damaging data being created throughout the course of the case. Attorneys can work with their clients to deactivate accounts both effectively and in ways that do not run the risk of violating any court orders or jurisdiction-specific laws about data retention, if any are applicable.

Social Media in Political Movements
by Ken Montenegro, Esq., Center for Constitutional Rights (CCR)

We can't escape the reality that social media is a factor in political movements. I believe we should approach its use from a place of power, not paranoia—in which each individual, group, or movement has clear objectives for why and how they're using it and are attuned to its risks. Each formation might reach a different conclusion about how they use social media. Social media use can be part of a wider media strategy to share information and events, lift up the courageous acts of our comrades, and demystify the invulnerability of our oppressors.

Social media use is not without risk, and larger social media platforms are antithetical to collective liberation. Thus, we should have conversations about social media through a lens of *harm reduction*. Examples include ensuring we practice good digital consent and not sharing footage that contains information that could be used to identify activists.

Conversations about surveillance can't begin and end with social media. We can extend our conversations about security culture and digital consent to give us broad, shared understandings; then, the specific issues around social media should fit into a security framework. Holistic approaches to security can shatter the false compartmentalization, uncertainty/fear, and reverence we have for the digital. Ultimately, these are conversations about what sacrifices we're making to reduce risks. Our use of any tool should be based on a thoughtful analysis of the risks and rewards of using tools designed to repress and surveil us.

If your client has a defense committee, it may opt to have an online presence to build support and solidarity. We urge defense committees to seek out up-to-date resources on the risks of social media and effective ways of reducing those risks when engaging those platforms to build political support for defendants. We also advise defense committees against any Internet presence that opens up a public forum in which comments, videos, or photos can be posted by the public; creating online spaces for material that could potentially be damaging to defendants generally does more harm than good because they give the government easy access to it.

Defense committees often choose to build websites as well, either hosted on readily available commercial servers, on private servers run by activist groups, or on individually run servers provided by a supporter. With any hosting platform, we suggest defense committees research the provider's terms of service, encryption setup, data retention policies (and what they do not log), and track-record for responding to government subpoenas. Websites often make their way into discovery, and the data in website logs can present liabilities to radical defendants, their supporters, and their movements.

2.0 Engaging With the Media From a Movement Perspective

The media might pay more attention to your client and their charges than they do to most criminal cases. The police and/or prosecution might be more inclined than usual to make use of the media in cases against radicals, such as by staging press conferences after raiding houses and arresting radicals, putting out press releases after filing charges, or making media statements after plea agreements or verdicts are announced that put their own spin on the legal outcome of the case. The police and prosecutors can be adept at using the media to help them gain control of the narrative and demonize your client and their political movements.

Likewise, mainstream media may follow the case closely and report on it in unfavorable ways that blast the accused or their movements. Or, they may follow the case closely and harshly criticize the police or prosecutor for the way they're handling the case. The coverage might be all over the place, or change drastically as more about the case comes to light through pretrial proceedings and the trial itself. No matter what happens in the public sphere, there may be more happening than attorneys are used to navigating. Tracking and keeping a file on media related to the case may be a useful task for someone on the defense committee.

With all this in mind, clients and their attorneys can consider how media engagement might impact the social and political movements of which clients are a part. We recommend that lawyers, their clients, and defense committees work together to figure out how (and if/when) to handle media and social media.

2.1 Taking a Strategic View of Media

Engaging with the media should not be seen as either inevitable or necessary, just as refusing to engage should not be seen as the best or only way to approach the case. Instead, media (including social media) is best conceived of as a strategic decision to help your client meet their overall goals for their case. As such, media is best seen not as a goal in and of itself, but as part of an overarching strategy to further your client's goals and resistance movements. When engaging with the media is desirable, preparing media strategies early on to help the pursuit of goals is best; the police and/or prosecution will likely waste no time with this, and clients' media strategies often need to play catch-up to combat the government's media efforts.

Media strategies and plans are generally most effective when they include details such as what will be said about different aspects of the case or the politics of the case (i.e., the talking points about the case), what will not be said, who will talk about which aspects and in which venues, and which media opportunities will be pursued or rejected. Developing these strategies and plans is outside the scope of this guide, but the resources we mentioned in Section 1.0 in this chapter are good places to start.

Likewise, a media plan should be adaptable as the case develops. There might be differences in how you, your client, or your client's defense committee interacts with the media depending on which stage of the case you are in (pretrial, trial, post-trial, et cetera). Section 3.0 in this chapter explores these considerations in more depth to help you figure out with your client how media does or does not fit into your legal strategy, based on your client's goals.

2.2 Pros and Cons of Media Engagement

Anything that people facing charges say in the media can be used against them, so that will always be a consideration for radical clients talking to the media. Some radicals may view engagement with mainstream media as undesirable for political reasons. Yet, there are many strategic reasons why it could be helpful to engage with the media, and people who can do so when you and your client choose not to.

The pros of engaging with the media include: countering the narrative put out by the police or prosecution; helping defendants feel supported by knowing that the public is aware of the case; promoting fundraising efforts; contributing to political pressure being applied to the prosecutor, politicians, or other decision makers; and turning public opinion against the political opponents of the movements that radical clients are part of. When radicals prioritize political gains over legal victories, they may be more interested in the pros of engaging with the media than in the potential consequences or liabilities of speaking out while their charges are pending. Likewise, they may want their defense committee to participate in media opportunities even if the attention that is created makes their legal situation more complicated.

There are also many potential drawbacks to media coverage. These will be obvious to most attorneys, whereas others might be more in the realm of political drawbacks. For example, controlling the media narrative can be an extraordinarily hard, time-consuming, and expensive ordeal, so prioritizing media tasks can drain your client's and a defense committee's energy and resources in ways that are detrimental to the overall support effort for your client. Radicals facing charges and defense committees may also find that the media coverage generated is not focused on the issues that they care about most, which could lead to politically unsatisfactory results even if the coverage itself is generally positive.

In cases against radicals, these pros and cons are much broader than in typical criminal defense cases, and evaluating the pros and cons is thus most effective from a broad view that considers the clients' legal, personal, and political goals as well as the interests and capacity of those who are supporting them.

2.3 Making Collaborative Decisions About Media

We want to emphasize the importance of decisions about media being made collaboratively between lawyers, clients, and (when applicable) defense committees. Whether or not to create media, or to respond to media narratives about the case, is often one of the most complicated and, at times, contentious aspects of repression against radicals. As a lawyer representing a radical client, you may find that considering strategic questions about media requires more of you than is typical in many criminal defense cases.

The decision of whether to prioritize media depends on both your client's goals and the specific circumstances of the case. For example, if one of your client's goals is to resolve the case quickly and with little fanfare, engaging with the media might be not be necessary, effective, or desirable. However, if your client wants to shift public opinion about the political circumstances surrounding their case, engaging with the media might be strategically necessary, even if doing so might complicate the legal strategy or add stress to defense preparations that might otherwise not exist.

If the circumstances or political environment surrounding the case are particularly charged, your client or their defense committee may feel a lot of pressure or urgency to speak to the media. The need to offer a counternarrative to the ugly picture the prosecution or police are painting might feel intensely compelling. If you feel that media will be detrimental to the legal defense or would unnecessarily complicate it, a lot of negotiation and compromise might be needed to determine an overall approach to handling the case that will work for both you and your client. Try to remember that media isn't usually an all or nothing proposition. For example, it is possible to put forth a narrative that aligns with your client's goals without having comments attributable to them.

Lawyers and their clients will benefit from open communication about media strategy and plans. Checking in with your client frequently about media strategy is useful, as the media environment can change quickly and evaluations of whether or not it is beneficial to talk with the media can change quickly as well. There may be times at which you need to also consider how the media strategy fits in with any applicable ethical rules you might be subject to. In general, including discussions of media strategy in your conversations with your client at each stage of the case can be an effective way of ensuring you are on the same page about media strategy and plans.

Collaborating on Media Strategy
by Moira Meltzer-Cohen, Esq.

Advising clients about media can present unique challenges. You must account for the clarity and accuracy of information put before the public, the credibility of your client's narrative with respect to their political goals, reducing your client's exposure to criminal (or future civil) liability, and antioppressive principles.

It must be made excruciatingly clear to your clients that any public statement attributed to them absolutely will be used against them. Reviewing written statements for accuracy and legal risk is a great way to help clients promote their narrative while minimizing the risks of harm.

Many radical defendants have strong feelings about "having their day in court." If what they need is to tell their story, resolving the case and mounting a media campaign instead of going to trial may make sense.

Consider the ways in which the public face of the case can affect both the case itself and your client's community and movements. It may or may not make sense for you or your client to be the spokesperson. Thus, consider principles of antioppression when developing media strategy in addition to ensuring your clients' narrative goals are effectively pursued.

2.4 Determining Who Speaks About What, and When

A common part of media plans is determining spokespeople who are well versed in talking points and who have experience or are willing to practice interacting with various types of media. If you are experienced in speaking with the media, this might be a role that you can play easily;

if this is new to you, there might be a considerable learning curve as you gain skills and become familiar with the talking points (and/or help determine what these talking points are). Likewise, your client or people affiliated with their defense committee might have a lot of experience and skills in engaging with the media, or they might be gaining media skills for the first time while dealing with all the stresses and uncertainties of resisting state repression. All of these are things to consider when choosing people to speak to the media.

Although many attorneys advise their clients not to speak to the media at all, some radical clients will want to speak for themselves, even when doing so might complicate their legal defense. Lawyers can assist their radical clients by informing them of the potential legal benefits and risks for speaking publicly on various topics (e.g., about the politics of the case but not the facts of the case or details of the indictment, et cetera).

Other common considerations about media spokespeople in political cases are whether potential spokespeople could be called as witnesses in the case (by either the defense or the prosecution), whether they could be charged in the future, or whether they have more valuable skill sets in other areas of support (paralegal skills, bookkeeping skills, et cetera). At times, potential spokespeople have public or social media presences/personas that could be beneficial, detrimental, or a combination of both; considering how someone's "celebrity" status could affect the way the talking points are received and how much attention is brought to the case can be an important part of deciding who will be a spokesperson. Many times, radicals will want to ensure that there is diversity among the spokespeople (e.g., not only white men speaking to the media). This may be especially important when the radical clients are people of color, gender-nonconforming or trans folks, et cetera. This also helps ensure that the unique experiences of people whose identities are marginalized are not further drowned out by people who have not experienced similar forms of oppression.

At times, it might make sense for you to be a spokesperson, even if you are only willing to speak about the legal aspects of the case and not the political ones. At other times, it might not make sense for you to be a spokesperson because of the considerations listed previously, because your speaking skills may be better applied in a court setting than in a media setting, or for other reasons. As with any other decision about spokespeople, the decision about whether you or any member of the legal team should be a spokesperson is best made in collaboration with the client. Always remember that you should not speak about your client without their permission. Be sure to consult with them about and honor the language they would like you to use when talking about their case. For example, a client arrested due to an antipipeline action might prefer to be described as a "water protector" rather than a "protester." Often there are well-thought-out, strategic reasons to use language that might at first seem strange or confusing.

Another common situation also bears mentioning: pressure campaigns conducted by defense committees or other supporters to try to get the charges reduced or dismissed. When pressure campaigns are used against the prosecutor or other political figures, the media environment or implications of engaging the media may be different than if media work is not being conducted in tandem with political organizing. For example, pressure campaigns involving media stunts, disruptions of political events featuring the politicians being pressured, satirical writings or videos, and so on could create opportunities for people opposed to your client, their supporters, or their movements to create drama in the media or online that may make being a spokesperson less desirable or more stressful. These situations also might make the legal aspects of the case more difficult, which can conflict with a lawyer's priorities for talking about cases publicly. When legal strategies and political strategies are operating simultaneously, the considerations about who speaks about what and when may be different than if only the legal side of the case is in play.

Finally, it can be beneficial to determine which spokesperson talks about which aspects of the case, and in which venues. For example, spokespeople might be well positioned to talk about the legal aspects of the case but not the political ones, or vice versa; other spokespeople might shine through in sympathetic media outlets but not do well when faced with adversarial reporters or with opponents in a debate-style interview, or vice versa. If the support effort is large enough to include several spokespeople, choosing who does which media tasks can be strategic and effective. Otherwise, deciding against certain media opportunities might be the most beneficial.

2.5 Representing the Politics of the Case With Integrity

A final point about media needs to be made before we dive into using media as part of an overall strategy: It is of utmost importance that media narratives about the case are both truthful and represent the politics of the case with integrity. Although defense attorneys or media spokespeople would not wittingly lie about the facts of a case, either in the court or in the media, it can be easy to talk about the politics of the case in disingenuous or misleading ways. This doesn't have to be malicious or intentional; it can be as simple as not understanding the radical client's politics, the political ramifications of the charges, or the ways in which state repression of radical political movements operates in the United States.

For example, media spokespeople might want to speak on the outrage of a teacher or member of the clergy facing prison time for civil disobedience at a pipeline construction site, whereas the person facing charges in that case might want the attention placed on the pipeline's contribution to environmental devastation. Similarly, if the person facing charges has a job that is generally respected by society, that aspect of their lives might not be the point or the reason the government is targeting them, so focusing on that aspect of the case might not accurately represent the politics of the case.

Many cases also involve allegations that may evoke strong emotional reactions from people, such as assault or murder charges, which might be unpleasant to discuss openly or challenging to talk about in ways that grapple with the complexities of the case. For example, a person of color facing assault or murder charges after defending themself from white supremacists might want the media strategy to analyze neo-fascist violence and the necessity of personal and community self-defense in the face of such attacks, but well-intentioned spokespeople might be tempted to advocate for nonviolence in the hopes of appealing to a broader swath of the general public.

Similarly, anarchists who face criminal charges for property destruction (e.g., smashing a bank window at a summit protest) may wish to take a militant and unapologetic stance in engagement with the media. Talking about cases with political integrity can be done in a way that does not jeopardize the potential for a favorable legal outcome. Anarchists have navigated these considerations in a variety of ways, from having defense committee affiliates speak publicly to putting out anonymous statements, to speaking openly about the larger issues surrounding the charges without commenting on the facts surrounding arrests. In any case, it is imperative that attorneys representing radicals in these scenarios make decisions about media collaboratively, and that your client's political positions and goals are given equal consideration as their legal goals.

3.0 Media Engagement to Support Client Goals

As mentioned previously, media is best seen as part of a strategy for pursuing a radical client's legal, personal, and political goals—but not as a goal in and of itself. When media creation and participation is desired, there are many decisions to make. These decisions will be specific to each individual case, but there are two broad principles to remember when developing a media strategy: 1) interact with media in ways that support political movements; and 2) guard against media harming others (e.g., codefendants, unindicted protesters, et cetera).

Radical clients may approach media from a movement perspective, rather than an individualistic perspective. In addition to wanting media to be part of the overarching approach to their case, they may want to try to get the media to help their movements or to help fight back against oppression or injustice. Accordingly, they may want anyone who speaks about their case to do so honestly and with integrity. This does not mean that anyone needs to speak in ways that might compromise your client's legal situation, and care can be given to ensure your client's political positions are respected while protecting the legal strategy.

For example, if your client has been entrapped by a government informant, it might be important to your client to counter the government's media narrative, either in mainstream media or through producing their own publications in movement media. Entrapment is a legally complicated defense, but in the public mind it might seem simpler and more straightforward. With that in mind, your client and/or their defense committee might focus on the repressive nature of government entrapment to shift the public opinion about your client's case, perhaps with the effect of influencing the prosecutor's decision to pursue charges.

To effectively combat the government's narrative, it will be important to coordinate efforts between everyone involved with or affected by the media strategy: you, your client, other clients and their lawyers, and members of the defense committee. Coming to agreements on how to talk—and not talk—about defendants and other radical arrestees in the media is an important part of developing a media strategy that supports resistance movements. Meeting directly with the defense committee to agree on talking points is one way to ensure cohesion. Thus, political cases involving a media strategy often call on lawyers to work with more people and in different ways than typical criminal defense cases. This work can be beneficial not only to the clients as individuals, but also to the movements that they are prioritizing along with (or more than) their own situations.

Effective media strategies can complement your client's goals for their case by acting as a real catalyst for building support and solidarity, bolstering political pressure campaigns, and fundraising for defense needs. The defense committee can be particularly helpful in creating and working towards these goals. For example, through strategic interviews and a well-developed media presence, the defense committee can help build a narrative around your client's case that results in broader and longer lasting support for your client, both from people actively involved in social movements and from those who are sympathetic to their movements. Visible support such as this can help strengthen movements and keep people facing charges feeling resilient in the face of state repression. Similarly, such robust support can minimize the harm that facing charges or getting convicted can bring by helping clients feel supported and connected throughout prison sentences.

In these ways, media strategies can be an important part of helping radicals pursue their political goals for their cases and of strengthening their movements. Thus, the second broad principle: not harming others through media participation. Being careful with talking points and other statements made in the media or over social media is a necessary part of ensuring that nothing is said that can directly or indirectly harm others, such as implicating unindicted radicals in ways that might make future charges more likely, making codefendants or unindicted radicals look like "bad protesters" or the "real criminals," implying (whether explicitly or implicitly) that certain actions—such as property destruction or sabotage—are more deserving of criminal prosecution while other forms of resistance are not, and so on.

3.1 Developing a Media Strategy

With these broad principles and your client's legal, personal, and political goals in mind, the ground will generally be laid for developing a media strategy and plan. How this is done will vary with each case, and how to go about this is outside the scope of this guide. Nevertheless, it's important to emphasize the benefits of everyone involved working to make collaborative decisions and create strategies, talking points, et cetera that everyone can agree on.

If you are supportive of the media strategy and interested in being an active part of it, you might be very involved in creating talking points, doing interviews, coaching media spokespeople on what is helpful and unhelpful to talk about in terms of the facts of the case and legal strategy, et cetera. Or, you might simply want to review any talking points, written interviews, recorded interviews, or press releases before publication to make sure they do not pose potentially negative consequences for the legal defense. You might also want to discuss the differences between talking about the facts of the case and the politics of the case with spokespeople before interviews to help everything go as smoothly as possible. Likewise, your client may want you to sign off on anything put out publicly but not want you to speak to the media yourself, or they may want you to sign off on anything that they say to the media but not be involved in media work that their defense committee does. Again, there are as many ways of developing and deploying a media strategy as there are cases.

It is worth noting that collaborative decision making doesn't mean everyone does the same thing. With a case involving multiple defendants who hold a variety of political positions or defendants spread out geographically, such as those arrested at a summit protest, there may be a wide variety of media that is put out through mainstream, independent, and movement channels. There can (and should!) be a diversity of voices and positions represented in these cases, and media engagement, creation, and participation will be enriched by taking a multifaceted approach. So long as all media creators engaged with the case are coming from a place of political integrity and do not knowingly harm others who are facing charges, a complementary approach of this sort will be greater than the sum of its parts. Similarly, if you, your client, and your client's defense committee are all engaging with the media in various ways, these efforts can be geared towards best serving your client and the resistance movements of which they are a part. These efforts can be more about working to not undermine each other than agreeing to do the same thing or make the same points, and drawing on each group or individual's skills, political position, and capacity.

Your job as an attorney will include advising your client of any potential legal repercussions of certain media engagement decisions. Even if you are not supportive of your client's desire to engage with the media, you and your client may need to come to an understanding of your differing perspectives and priorities and continue to advise them accordingly.

3.2 Adapting Media Strategy as the Case Develops

As you, your client, and the defense committee develop the media strategy, it's important to consider the ways in which it might change over time. Changes become necessary in response to developments in the case that are outside of the defense's control, such as whistleblowers leaking information related to the case, prosecution witnesses becoming embroiled in scandals that open political opportunities for media engagement, shifting narratives in the media, the judge issuing an unexpected ruling that drastically changes the legal landscape of the case, et cetera. Remaining adaptable to changes in media strategy, talking points, approaches to interviews, and so on is an important part of executing media strategies in political cases.

There are also landmarks within criminal cases that lend themselves to different media strategies or plans, or that have different implications for how media strategies are developed. As the lawyer, you are likely well positioned to help your client and their supporters anticipate the different stages of the pending case and prepare their media strategy in ways that help pursue client goals without unnecessarily complicating the legal defense. For example, there may be talking points about the case that are only appropriate after an affirmative defense is specified, such as not talking about a client facing an "assault on an officer" charge as having acted in self-defense until self-defense is decided upon as the affirmative defense. Anyone sympathetic to the person facing charges may automatically talk about the case as one of self-defense against a violent cop, but it may not be strategic or advantageous to the person facing charges for their media spokespeople or for you as their lawyer to do so if that could conflict with or detract from the legal defense chosen down the line. In this way, there are times when the legal strategy may need to lead the media strategy, or at least inform it so that no easily avoidable conflicts spring up along the way.

Similarly, if a client is convicted or pleads guilty and has to wait for the sentencing hearing, there may be an interim period between when the case feels like it's over on an emotional level and when it's actually closed on a legal level. When there are still open questions about what the consequences for the client will be, it may be in the client's best interests, for example, to hold off on talking points that challenge the legitimacy of the government to incarcerate people at all or the necessity of physically resisting police brutality. Again, it might be up to you to explain the legal implications of media decisions at these still-critical points of a client's case if your client or the defense committee are not as familiar with the criminal legal system. What is in the client's best interests ultimately depends on their overall goals for their case, not just their legal best interests, but understanding the legal landmarks within the criminal case can help inform decisions about media strategy.

After sentences are handed down, the considerations about what is strategic to say or not say can often change drastically. As the lawyer, your role in the media effort may or may not end at this point. Similarly, the client's situation may or may not change in ways that make them feel more at liberty to speak their mind about the case or the politics of the case; if they're planning to appeal their conviction, for example, they might consider their situation and media strategy to be mostly unchanged, whereas they might speak freely despite the risks of further repression if they're expecting to just serve their time and then move on. Whatever happens, having clear, intentional discussions at each stage of the case will be beneficial.

3.3 Maintaining a Cohesive Media Narrative

In addition to thinking of the media strategy as a constantly evolving endeavor, thinking of it as a working relationship that goes beyond the traditional attorney-client dynamic can be helpful. This is especially true when defense committees engage the media, as discussed in the following subsection. When there are multiple defendants in cases, this can also include coordinating between all the defendants and their lawyers, balancing each defendant's individual goals and priorities, and coordinating with the defendants' various defense committees or other support structures.

To maintain a cohesive narrative, your client and/or their defense committee might ask you to review media materials so you can alert them to any potential legal pitfalls. It might feel like this isn't your job, but it can help you avoid complicated legal situations later. If you are transparent about the process and rationale for your suggested revisions, omissions, or additions, you can aid the media efforts, help your client meet all their goals for their case, and maintain a strong working relationship with their political support.

When engaging the media, it's important to coordinate efforts between you, all the defendants involved, other lawyers on the case, and defense committees. However, this doesn't necessarily mean that media narratives are monolithic, centralized, or controlled by any one particular individual or group, particularly when there are disagreements about strategies and goals. Effective coordination looks like open communication about shared principles and care taken so that those facing charges do not have their political positions compromised or their legal strategies put at risk. Coordinating media efforts while allowing for creativity and initiative provides opportunities for ensuring that all media efforts are supportive of your client, any codefendants, and others who are a part of their resistance movements.

3.4 Defense Committees and the Media

We covered defense committees in detail in chapter 4, yet a brief look here is needed. Defense committees can be an invaluable part of creating a robust defense for your client and can conduct media efforts in ways that clients and defense attorneys cannot or do not want to. In addition to potentially having people with media skills that clients or lawyers do not have, defense committees may have members whose political ideas and experiences can add nuance and creative content to a media narrative. Media spokespeople may also be better positioned to take a militant stance in talking points that clients or lawyers are not well positioned to take; for example, they could speak critically about the criminal legal system, the prison-industrial complex, police brutality, or environmental devastation in ways that may risk political fall-out but not sanctions from the judge. Additionally, they may be able to do the majority or entirety of the media work and create an overall benefit for your client without you or your client needing to expend your limited time and resources on this aspect of the case.

4.0 Common Situations and Areas of Tension

There are a couple of common situations and areas of tension that require more exploration: solidarity actions and resolving disagreements.

4.1 Solidarity Actions

A common way of showing solidarity with radicals facing charges is solidarity actions, which frequently happen across the world and are often shared via social media. Many of these actions are legal in most countries, such as group photos with banners and signs. In certain jurisdictions or countries, however, these actions might be illegal, such as places that criminalize wearing masks or face coverings in public. Other actions might be generally illegal, such as dropping banners off freeway overpasses or high-rise buildings, wheat-pasting flyers on walls and street posts, graffiti, placing stickers on public or private property, or sabotaging construction equipment or other privately owned equipment.

Solidarity actions are generally conducted autonomously by people around the world who are sympathetic to the politics of the case or opposed to the repression that the activists involved in your client's case are facing. Although calls for solidarity are frequently made by defense committees, there are often no pre-existing relationships between radicals facing charges and the people across the world who organize or participate in solidarity actions in support of their fights against state repression, much less coordination, planning involving your client, or instructions from your client for others to carry out potentially illegal activities.

The prosecution may try to use these unconnected actions to vilify your client. Be prepared for situations such as this, and talk to media spokespeople about it. If you are also engaging with the media, you should be prepared to address the relevant political talking points about the case when attention is given to solidarity actions, or to redirect the interview to the legal talking points you want to address.

4.2 Resolving Disagreements

Because criminal charges often carry high stakes and lead to emotionally charged situations, it's common for disagreements to occasionally arise. These disagreements can unfortunately be quite challenging. No matter how minor or major the disagreement, however, it's important that internal disagreements, conflicts, and disputes remain internal. Even if you don't feel like you are a part of the political organizing effort that is supporting your client, it can be important to consider handling disagreements with your client's comrades in similar ways that you would handle disagreements or conflicting priorities with your client. Although this does not mean that defense committee members have an attorney-client relationship with you, this does mean, for example, that it is best not to air grievances or disputes with your client's defense committee or other supporters in public venues, just as you would not go to the media with a disagreement you were having with your client.

A good rule to keep in mind is that disagreements with the defense committee or other supporters should never be aired in the media or over social media. Airing internal conflict publicly often does more to embolden and empower the prosecution or other opponents than it does to resolve the conflicts, and places more stress on people facing charges. As with any media interaction, sticking to the points you want to make to further your client's goals will ultimately be more effective than taking that opportunity to speak publicly about conflicts, tension, bad blood, et cetera. Likewise, as the attorney, you should be able to trust that your client and their supporters will not use public forums to air disagreements they have with you.

Conclusion

We started this book with two fundamental premises in mind: 1) lawyers can work with their radical clients as peers in shared struggle to provide them with a robust criminal defense that understands their best interests to include all their goal areas and the strength of their movements as well; and 2) radicals facing criminal charges can approach their criminal cases with legal, personal, and political goals in mind, and with a focus on making the best decisions for both themselves and their movements as a whole. We also approached the ideas in this book with the aim of transforming the process of fighting criminal charges into something that can strengthen and embolden our social movements rather than weaken them.

Throughout the book, we tried to avoid giving prescriptive advice, instead posing questions, offering suggestions, and making observations about how movement attorneys have approached their litigation in the past and about how radical clients tend to approach their cases. For much of the book, we imagined adding our thoughts into an ongoing conversation among lawyers with interest and/

or experience in representing radicals, as you are the ones immersed in your profession, with all its advantages and limitations. We hope that the arguments and proposals we have made here have helped reinvigorate and/or open new ways of thinking for all our readers.

Part of the transformation that both this guide and *A Tilted Guide to Being a Defendant* seek to accomplish is a cultural shift in the ways that anyone involved in radical social movements in the so-called United States handles criminal charges. This is necessarily a multifaceted shift, requiring innovation, creativity, resistance, and rebellion from lawyers, legal workers, radical clients, and everyone who supports all the people who are involved in resisting state repression while fighting for a better world. We only aspire to this book being a small part of that process of transformation. We believe that we can collectively find ways of dealing with the brutally repressive mechanisms of the criminal legal system and prison-industrial complex that will strengthen our movements for social justice and liberation.

Lawyers have played many important roles in these struggles over the decades and will, of necessity, continue to. The quickly shifting legal landscape in so many areas—conspiracy laws, terrorism laws, immigration laws, surveillance, and data/biometrics collection, among others—points to the increasing need for movement attorneys. Radical social movements quite earnestly need radical attorneys (and attorneys in solidarity with radicals).

We believe that attorneys can figure out ways to support radical clients that provide them with the strongest possible representation to the benefit of everyone involved in those struggles. And although we have presented many ideas, suggestions, and recommendations throughout this book, you will ultimately be the ones who break the ground necessary to fully realize what it can mean for attorneys to be in solidarity with radicals and radical social movements. We hope these ideas are a useful contribution to the work you'll be doing.

Acknowledgments

Tilted Scales is a small collective of anarchist legal workers who have spent years supporting and fighting for radical people facing charges, prisoners, **political prisoners, prisoners of war**, and **politicized prisoners**. Our legal **solidarity** efforts have involved support during all stages of a person's case—from arrest through trial and into postconviction appeals and long-term prison support. We offer workshops, webinars, and discussions about the criminal legal system and the ideas presented in our publications to people facing charges and their supporters. We also collaborate with attorneys while doing political support work for defendants and their communities; this book draws heavily on those experiences and the perspectives we've gained over the years.

This book has been a long time in the making. Since the seed for it was planted in 2012, countless individuals have contributed to its growth and fruition. Our desires to write collectively and to incorporate feedback over the years from prisoners, lawyers, legal workers, friends, and comrades have meant a slower process, but a better one. We tried our best to include perspectives from a multitude of people with all different kinds of experience with the criminal legal system.

This book is also a result of the accumulated collective wisdom of attorneys, legal workers, and radicals who've faced charges across the country who shared with us their thoughts on representing radicals in ways that strengthen movements for social justice and liberation while simultaneously mounting solid legal defenses. Many also shared their feedback as this book went through various drafts to the book in front of you today.

We would like to thank these people for taking time to review our drafts and for their thoughtful feedback and contributions: Amreet Sandhu, Andrew Plasse and Ramsey Orta's support crew, Azadeh Shahshahani and Project South, Ben Rosenfeld, Bob, Cedar, Cindy Milstein, Colleen Flynn, Dennis Cunningham, the Electronic Frontier Foundation (EFF), Elisa Y. Lee, Ella, Garrett Fitzgerald, Jan Susler, Jeffrey Haas, Jordan Winquist, Ken Montenegro, Lauren Regan and the Civil Liberties Defense Center (CLDC), Leslie James Pickering, Lisa Drapkin, Lori Black Bear, Luce Guillén-Givins, Margaret Killjoy, Marguerite, Mark Bray, Mark Vermeulen, Meghsha Sqawsan Barner, Michael Deutsch, Michael Loadenthal, Michele Gretes, Moira Meltzer-Cohen, Molly Armour, Nick Zotos, Nikita, Pooja Gehi and the National Lawyers Guild (NLG), Rachel Lederman, Rachel Rosnick, Rae, Tasha Moro, Tim Phillips, Traci Yoder, Tyler Ingraham, Wade Rosenthal, and Walter Riley. And an especial thanks to Betsy Raasch-Gilman, former member of Tilted Scales, for helping write the initial outline years ago and providing feedback as the book itself came into being.

We would also like to thank Kristian Williams and Sarah Coffey for their editorial assistance, keen political insight, and friendship. Likewise, many thanks to Kris Hermes for detailed copyediting of our final draft. Thanks to Institute for Anarchist Studies and AK Press for believing in this project and for helping us see it through. And to the countless others who offered encouragement and support for what they believed to be a useful resource for our struggles and movements, our sincerest thanks.

Most importantly, this book is inspired by the strength and courage of the prisoners who continue to struggle on the inside, every day.

Glossary

Agent provocateur: An infiltrator into a political group, organization, or movement, often at the behest of a governmental organization or private entity, who intends to provoke individuals and groups into taking illegal action.

Agent suppressant: An infiltrator whose goals typically include gathering information and creating conditions that prevent the group from organizing effectively (stirring up drama, invoking bureaucratic roadblocks to stall progress, sabotaging projects and activities).

Anarchist: People who ascribe to a political theory that aims to create a society without political, economic, or social hierarchies. Anarchists struggle towards the maximization of individual liberty and social cooperation in their political projects, interpersonal relationships, and day-to-day activities. Common tenants of anarchism include mutual aid, direct action, and autonomy. Anarchists often support a diversity of tactics in the struggle for social change, including militant tactics and illegality.

Anticapitalist: A person who opposes capitalism, globalization, and the social roles and relationships produced by each (worker, boss, et cetera).

Antifascist ("antifa"): A person or group who is opposed to fascism and the rise of neo-fascism; a multifaceted and militant political framework of social revolutionism to dismantle the far right that relies on a variety of tactics. See Mark Bray, *Antifa: The Anti-Fascist Handbook* (New York: Melville House Publishing, 2017).

Assigned gender: The gender declared for people, generally at birth and on state-issued birth documentation, based on the discretion of the medical personnel or other person completing the paperwork; the gender designation is typically based on visible sex characteristics (male or female anatomy in a binary understanding of both sex and gender).

Cisgender (or cis): A person whose sense of gender identity corresponds with the anatomical sex they were assigned at birth.

Comrade: A highly political term to describe people involved in shared political struggles; we sometimes use it interchangeably with "peer" when referring to lawyers and defendants working together.

Criminal legal system: A term to describe what is commonly called the "criminal justice system" without endorsing the myth that this system provides justice, instead focusing on how it is a legal system for criminalizing actions, ideas, associations, people, and communities, as well as for determining punishments for people deemed to have broken the laws created by the government.

Defense committee: A shorthand term to refer to any group of friends, family, and/or supporters of defendants who do fundraising, legal and court support, direct personal support, and political support on behalf of defendants, generally with a focus on the political and social issues surrounding the case.

Gender nonconforming/genderqueer: A broad identity term used by people who do not subscribe to gender expressions or roles expected of them by society based on their assigned gender. These terms may also be used by people whose gender identity or expression is outside of the male/female binary, or who understand their identity to be a combination of genders, or no gender at all.

Innocence politics: Calls for justice that are contingent upon appeals to notions of respectability and the assumption that defendants are not guilty of the charges they are facing.

Intersex: An umbrella term used for a variety of conditions in which a person is born with or develops (without medical intervention) primary or secondary sex characteristics that do not fit into a rigid male/female binary. Such developments may be apparent at birth or identified in puberty or adulthood. It is a socially constructed category that reflects biological variation.

Jailhouse lawyer: A prisoner who navigates the criminal and/or civil legal system, usually as a self-taught legal advocate, either for themselves or in support of others.

Legal collective: An organization composed of volunteer legal workers and/or attorneys that supports individuals, communities, and events (e.g., protests). A legal collective might coordinate "Know Your Rights" trainings, organize arrestees, collaborate with attorneys to provide jail and court support, and/or produce written materials on related topics. Also called "law collective."

Legal defense: Criminal defense that attorneys develop with and for their clients.

Legal goals: Goals set around the legal strategy that focus on and prioritize the legal components of a case (as opposed to personal or political aspects).

Legal worker: Anyone who participates in antirepression organizing and/or with aspects of the criminal or civil legal systems who does not have an active bar card; includes paralegals, investigators, administrative staff in law offices, activists working to change or otherwise affect legal systems, and radicals supporting named parties through the legal process.

Liberation: A term we often use to refer to politics that call for a fundamental change in the way that society is organized and that power is exercised. For many radicals, this means the abolition of the nation-state and all forms of hierarchy; for others, it means changing the political power structures from capitalist to socialist or communist structures.

Movement: A term used to describe a social phenomenon in which a large number of people across a political spectrum and geographical area mobilize in different ways around shared goals, generally using a range of tactics (Occupy Wall Street, the antiapartheid movement in South Africa, the Black liberation movement, the antiglobalization movement, et cetera).

Movement attorney: An attorney who has a radical political analysis, and approaches their work as a vehicle for social change.

Movement media: Media created by radicals, for radicals. The individuals and collectives who run these media outlets (e.g., websites, podcasts, radio shows, magazines, et cetera) will generally be the most willing to help your client and their cause.

Movement perspective: A term we use to describe a view of legal situations that weighs the best interests of a social movement with the best interests of the individual defendant.

Noncooperating plea agreement: A plea agreement that does not implicate others in any form, including any testimony given, the statement of facts, or in sentencing statements. These can include a clause that says the defendant will not be called to testify against others in the future.

Participatory defense: A community-organizing model for people facing charges, their families, and their communities to impact the outcomes of cases and transform the landscape of power in the court system by relying on the strengths and skills inherent in a defendant's family and community. This model sees families and communities as agents of change rather than service recipients, and asserts that they can make systemic change by engaging with their loved ones' criminal cases through community organizing. See participatorydefense.org.

Personal goals: Goals focused on helping a defendant care for themselves and their loved ones (e.g., avoiding prison time). These considerations include health status, children and other dependents, one's role in organizations/political movements, financial situations, immigration status, et cetera.

Political defense: A defense used in the courtroom, in the public sphere, or both, which prioritizes or emphasizes a defendant's politics or the political issues surrounding the case. Depending on the client, this may outweigh considerations about the legal outcome of the case.

Political goals: Goals created for and focused on the politics and ideas a defendant hopes to advance through the process of fighting their charges and/or bringing their case to trial.

Political pressure campaign: A term we use as a catch-all to describe political organizing directed at governmental decision makers or entities in support of defendants, or about the issues surrounding cases against radicals. Examples include media campaigns to mount pressure against prosecutors to drop the charges, political actions taken against companies who were being protested when arrests happened, and call-in campaigns against jails to ensure incarcerated defendants receive adequate healthcare.

Political prisoner: A person who is incarcerated after being identified as a threat to the ruling power structures and social order, and who considers their incarceration to be an act of political repression.

Politicized prisoner: A prisoner who develops a political analysis, often a radical one, while incarcerated, and aligns themselves with movements for social justice or liberation.

Political prosecution: A case in which charges are filed due to a defendant's (alleged) political beliefs, actions, and/or associations; the charges may be an effort to restrict or prevent the targeted individual's ability to remain politically active in their movement, create a chilling effect on the movement as a whole, punish anyone who challenges the dominant social order, scare others from challenging that order, et cetera.

Prison-industrial complex: A term used to describe the interconnections between state-run and private carceral systems, particularly in relation to the rise of mass incarceration in the United States. See Angela Davis, "Masked Racism: Reflections on the Prison Industrial Complex," September 10, 1998, https://www.colorlines.com/articles/masked-racism-reflections-prison-industrial-complex.

Prisoners of war: A term chosen by prisoners who do not recognize the legitimacy of the US court system; for example, certain Puerto Rican independence fighters (*independentistas*) and members of the Black Liberation Army (BLA). Other prisoners will choose this term because they see their charges as part of class war or social war.

People facing charges: A term we often use as an alternative to "defendants."

Queer: A broad sexual and gender identity often used to refer to people whose sexual and/or gender identity, sexual preferences, and/or sexual practices deviate from or oppose normative sexuality and/or relationship models.

Social justice: A concept of fair and equitable relations between all members of society often used in the context of addressing injustices, righting wrongs, and changing or abolishing social structures that create inequality, inequity, and oppression.

Solidarity: A political principle and belief that asserts there are shared interests between individuals/groups/ classes that are the basis for collaboration, coordination, and interdependence.

Snitch: (n.) a person who provides a governmental agency or private enterprise with information about another person, group, or organization; (v.) the act of providing information about another person, group, or organization to a governmental agency or private enterprise.

Systemic oppression: A term describing the governmental, economic, social, and cultural institutions and policies that create and maintain coercive hierarchies based on race, ethnicity, class, gender, physical abilities, nationality, or other identity markers.

Transgender: An adjective used most often as an umbrella term, and frequently shortened to "trans," describing a wide range of identities and experiences of people whose gender identity and/or expression differs from those that may be culturally expected based on their assigned sex at birth. Not all trans people seek gender-affirming interventions (such as hormones or surgery), nor do all gender rebels identify as trans. Common terms used at the time of this publication are: nonbinary, gender nonconforming, genderqueer, trans, feminine/masculine of center, and gender fluid.

Trauma-informed framework: A model for engaging with clients that promotes a culture of safety, empowerment, and healing, and that considers past trauma and resulting coping mechanisms when attempting to determine how to cultivate a beneficial professional–client relationship.

Notes

Foreword

1   Flynn McRoberts, "Oregon City is Cradle to Latest Generation of Anarchist Protesters," *Chicago Tribune*, August 12, 2000, https://www.chicagotribune.com/news/ct-xpm-2000-08-12-0008120203-story.html.

2   The "Green Scare" refers to a wave of repression that targeted animal and earth liberation movements following 9/11. Environmental activists—especially those who engaged in direct action—were cast by the state and mainstream media as "terrorists" and many were sentenced using terrorism enhancements.

3   The Earth Liberation Front and Animal Liberation Front were unconnected individuals or autonomous groups who took direct action to stop the exploitation and destruction of the earth and animals. "Operation Backfire" was a large policing operation across several states targeting people alleged to have participated in these movements' activities.

4   SLAPP stands for "strategic lawsuits against public participation."

Introduction

1   Wendy Sawyer and Peter Wagner, "Mass Incarceration: The Whole Pie," Prison Policy Initiative, March 19, 2019, https://www.prisonpolicy.org/reports/pie2019.html.

2   Tilted Scales Collective, *A Tilted Guide to Being a Defendant* (New York: Combustion Books, 2017).

Chapter 1: Representing Radical Clients

1   Importantly, although people with fascist, ultraconservative, "far right," "alt-right," oppressive, bigoted ideas and actions may desire a significant change in social order and may describe themselves as radicals, we must be clear that we do not endorse or support their ideologies, and do not act in solidarity with them.

2   We often use "they/them/their/theirs" when referring to individuals as a gender-neutral pronoun, in contrast to "he/him/his" or "she/her/hers."

3   A full exploration of various political approaches to fighting charges and/or using trials that challenge the legitimacy of the court or government is outside the scope of this book, but we provide examples in *A Tilted Guide to Being a Defendant*.

Chapter 2: Common Situations in Cases against Radicals

1   Brady violations occur when the prosecution suppresses evidence favorable to a defendant who has requested it. See Brady v. Maryland, 373 U.S. 83 (1963).

2   Memorandum from the Director, FBI to SAC, Albany (New York; routed simultaneously to 22 other field offices) dated August 25, 1967 and captioned COUNTERINTELLIGENCE

PROGRAM, BLACK NATIONALIST – HATE GROUPS, INTERNAL SECURITY. Cited in Ward Churchill and Jim Vander Wall, *Agents of Repression: The FBI's Secret Wars Against the Black Panther Party and the American Indian Movement* (Cambridge, MA: South End Press, 2002), 58.

3   See Trevor Aaronson, *The Terror Factory: Inside the FBI's Manufactured War on Terrorism* (Brooklyn: Ig Publishing, 2013); Jeffrey Haas, *The Assassination of Fred Hampton* (Brooklyn: Lawrence Hill Books, 2011); The Muslim American Civil Liberties Coalition (MACLC), The Creating Law Enforcement Accountability & Responsibility (CLEAR), and The Asian American Legal Defense and Education Fund (AALDEF), "Mapping Muslims: NYPD Spying and Its Impact on American Muslims," https://www.law.cuny.edu/wp-content/uploads/page-assets/academics/clinics/immigration/clear/Mapping-Muslims.pdf; Will Potter, *Green is the New Red: An Insider's Account of a Social Movement Under Siege* (San Francisco: City Lights Books, 2011).

4   The judge gave the jury conflicting oral and written responses to a question about the time frame for predisposition and whether Anna was an "agent." The defense did not know of this discrepancy until after the verdict was returned.

5   Rikki Klieman, John Thomas, and National Lawyers Guild, *Representation of Witnesses Before Federal Grand Juries* (Eagan, MN: Thomson Reuters, 2019).

6   "Grand jury," Wikipedia, https://en.wikipedia.org/wiki/Grand_jury#By_jurisdiction.

7   "Doxxing" (or "doxing") is slang for publicly releasing information about individuals.

8   This is not to say that radicals are the only people who take a strong stance of noncooperation. Many people refuse to

cooperate with the government for many reasons, including protecting loved ones, loyalty to others, personal convictions, and fear of worse consequences from others than from the government.

9   "Stonewall Riot Police Reports," OutHistory.org, http://outhistory.org/exhibits/show/stonewall-riot-police-reports.

10   Michael Loadenthal, "Now That Was A Riot!: Social Control in Felonious Times," *Global Society* 34, no. 1 (2020): 128–44.

11   S. 3880 (109th): Animal Enterprise Terrorism Act, November 15, 2006, https://www.govtrack.us/congress/bills/109/s3880/text.

12   Nancy Hollander, "The Holy Land Foundation Case: The Collapse of American Justice," *Washington and Lee Journal of Civil Rights and Social Justice* 20, no. 1 (2014): 45–61.

13   18 U.S. Code §2332b(g)(5)(A).

14   See Daniel McGowan, "Exposing 'Little Guantanamo:' Inside the CMU," Spring 2009, https://www.prisonlegalnews.org/media/publications/mcgowan_exposing_little_guantanamo_cmu_report_2009.pdf; Will Potter, "Communications Management Units," http://willpotter.com/CMU.

15   Bill Information for HB 1123, Oklahoma Legislature, https://legiscan.com/OK/text/HB1123/2017.

16   Alleen Brown, "Trump Administration Asks Congress to Make Disrupting Pipeline Construction a Crime Punishable by 20 Years in Prison," *The Intercept*, June 5, 2019, https://theintercept.com/2019/06/05/pipeline-protests-proposed-legislation-phmsa-alec.

17   "Legal Resources," Public Participation Project, https://anti-slapp.org/legal-resources.

18   See Jan Herman, "Leonard Weinglass, Our 'Modern Clarence Darrow,'" Straight Up | Herman: Arts, Media & Culture News with 'tude, September 6, 2016, https://www.artsjournal.com/herman/2016/09/leonard-weinglass-our-modern-clarence-darrow.html; Michael Steven Smith, *Lawyers for the Left: In the Courts, in the Streets, and on the Air* (New York: OR Books, 2019).

19   "The Climate Necessity Defense: A Legal Tool for Climate Activists," Climate Disobedience Center, http://www .climatedisobedience.org/necessitydefense.

20   See "Climate Necessity Defense Guide: A Guide for Activists and Attorneys," Climate Defense Project, March 28, 2019, http://climatedefenseproject.org/wp-content/uploads/2019/03/CDP-Climate-Necessity-Defense-Case-Guide-March-28-2019 .pdf; and William P. Quigley, "The Necessity Defense in Civil Disobedience Cases: Bring in the Jury," *New England Law Review* 38, no. 1 (2003): 3–72.

21   See Trevor Aaronson, *The Terror Factory* (New York: Ig Publishing, 2013); and a radio program about an FBI informant who targeted young Muslim men and exploited women in Orange County, California: "The Convert," *This American Life*, August 10, 2012, https://www.thisamericanlife.org/471/the-convert.

22   Jesse J. Norris and Hanna Grol-Prokopczyk, "Estimating the Prevalence of Entrapment in Post-9/11 Terrorism Cases," *Journal of Criminal Law and Criminology* 105, no. 3 (2015): 609–78.

23   People v. Ross II (2007) 155 Cal.App.4th 1033, 1045 (66 Cal.Rptr.3d 438).

24   See the example on our website: https://tiltedscalescollective.org/legal-resources/sample-joint-defense-agreement.

25   The American Bar Association states in Rule 21 of the Model Rules of Professional Conduct: "In representing a client, a lawyer shall exercise independent professional judgment and render candid advice. In rendering advice, a lawyer may refer not only to law but to other considerations such as moral, economic, social and political factors that may be relevant to the client's situation." See "Rule 2.1: Advisor," American Bar Association, https://www.americanbar.org/groups/professional_responsibility/publications/model_rules_of_professional_conduct/rule_2_1_advisor.

Chapter 3: Working with Radical Clients

1   Sample Representation Agreement, https://tiltedscale-scollective.org/legal-resources/sample-representation-agreement/

2   "Systems of Inequality: Criminal 'In'Justice," Sylvia Rivera Law Project, https://srlp.org/wp-content/uploads/2017/03/Disproportionate-Incarceration-Flowchart.pdf.

3   "Supporting Incarcerated Transgender and Non-Conforming People: A Tip Sheet for Attorneys and Advocates," Sylvia Rivera Law Project, https://srlp.org/wp-content/uploads/2017/01/supporting-incarcerated-tgnci-people-en-color.pdf.

4   See Smith, *Lawyers for the Left*.

Chapter 4: Working with Political Support

1   See Marcus Rediker, *The Amistad Rebellion: An Atlantic Odyssey of Slavery and Freedom* (New York: Viking, 2012).

2   Video can be one such useful resource, but it can also be harmful. If lawyers or defendants have it, they may be required to turn it over to the prosecution. In the past, activists have collected

and reviewed video footage and provided some of it to defense attorneys for their purposes without turning over the entirety of what they collected.

Institute for Anarchist Studies

The Institute for Anarchist Studies (IAS) was founded in 1996 and seeks to further antiauthoritarian thought by supporting the work of radical writers, filmmakers, and podcasters. We offer editorial mentorship, working closely with new and established writers to develop their ideas and voices for a general audience, as well as online and print publication opportunities: our website and social media presence; our annual journal, *Perspectives on Anarchist Theory*; and our various book series (published in partnership with AK Press). We also sponsor speakers, performances, and theory tracks at conferences and other public events. We fund leftist thinkers and culture makers, and prioritize creators of minority identities and those who operate outside of academia and therefore have less access to intellectual or material resources. When possible, we give grants to promote work that could not otherwise be made.

For more about the IAS, visit: anarchiststudies.org.

AK Press

AK Press is a worker-run collective that publishes and distributes radical books, visual and audio media, and other material. We work long hours for short money because we believe in what we do. We're anarchists, which is reflected both in the books we provide and the way we organize our business. Decisions at AK Press are made collectively, from what we publish, to what we distribute, and how we structure our labor. The work, from sweeping floors to answering phones, is shared. When the telemarketers call and ask, "who's in charge?" the answer is: everyone. Our goal is supplying radical words and images to as many people as possible. We ensure these materials are widely available to help you make positive (or hell, revolutionary) changes in the world. For more information on AK Press, or to place an order, see www.akpress.org.

Justseeds Artists' Cooperative

Justseeds Artists' Cooperative is a decentralized community of twenty-nine artists who have banded together to distribute their work as well as collaborate with and support each other. We regularly produce graphics and culture for social justice movements, much of which we distribute for free on our website. We believe in the power of personal expression in concert with collective action to transform society. For more information on Justseeds Artists' Cooperative or to order work, see www.justseeds.org.

Anarchist Interventions Series

AK PRESS is small, in terms of staff and resources, but we also manage to be one of the world's most productive anarchist publishing houses. We publish close to twenty books every year, and distribute thousands of other titles published by like-minded independent presses and projects from around the globe. We're entirely worker run and democratically managed. We operate without a corporate structure—no boss, no managers, no bullshit.

The **FRIENDS OF AK PRESS** program is a way you can directly contribute to the continued existence of AK Press, and ensure that we're able to keep publishing books like this one! Friends pay $25 a month directly into our publishing account ($30 for Canada, $35 for international), and receive a copy of every book AK Press publishes for the duration of their membership! Friends also receive a discount on anything they order from our website or buy at a table: 50% on AK titles, and 30% on everything else. We have a Friends of AK ebook program as well: $15 a month gets you an electronic copy of every book we publish for the duration of your membership. *You can even sponsor a very discounted membership for someone in prison.*

Email **friendsofak@akpress.org** for more info, or visit the website: **https://www.akpress.org/friends.html**.

There are always great book projects in the works—so sign up now to become a Friend of AK Press, and let the presses roll!